The Disciples' Prayer

The

Disciples'

Prayer

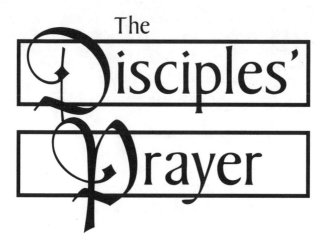

*An Intimate
Phrase by Phrase
Journey through
the Lord's Prayer*

Donald T. Williams

Christian Publications
CAMP HILL, PENNSYLVANIA

Christian Publications, Inc.
3825 Hartzdale Drive
Camp Hill, PA 17011
www.cpi-horizon.com

Faithful, biblical publishing since 1883

ISBN: 0-87509-764-2
© 1999 by Christian Publications, Inc.
All rights reserved
Printed in the United States of America

99 00 01 02 03   5 4 3 2 1

To my parents,
Thomas J. and Vera Lee Williams,
who have prayed for me and before me
for over forty years.

Contents

Sonnet XLIV: Ascriptions

Shepherd of stars and winds and ocean waves,
Watcher of sparrows, Numberer of hairs,
Fierce Flinger forth of lightning flares,
Mountain Molder, Carver-out of caves,
Smoke of Sinai, Setter-free of slaves,
Grain Gatherer, Burner-up of Tares,
God alone who sees, alone who cares,
Life Giver, Opener of Graves—

Our language lacks the necessary words,
Our minds the wit to sing your praise aright:
Inhabiter of hearts and vaulted naves,
Mighty Warrior, Healer, Lord who girds
His waist with righteousness, whose Life is light,
God alone who lives, alone who saves.

— D.T.W.

"After This Manner"

Prayer, the Church's banquet, Angel's age,
God's breath in man returning to his birth,
The soul in paraphrase, heart in pilgrimage,
The Christian plummet sounding heaven
and earth;
Engine against the Almighty, sinner's tower,
Reversed thunder, Christ-side-piercing spear,
The six-day's world transposing in an hour,
A kind of tune which all things hear and fear;
Softness and peace, and joy, and love, and bliss,
Exalted manna, gladness of the best,
Heaven in ordinary, man well dressed,
The milky way, the bird of Paradise,
Church bells beyond the stars heard,
the soul's blood,
The land of spices; something understood.
                    —George Herbert, from *The Temple*

"**U**h, Lord, thank You for this day, and, uh, forgive me for all my sins, Lord, and help me to get that job, Lord, if it's Your will. And please help John's cold to get better, Lord, and help me not to catch it. And, uh, oh yeah, please bless all the missionaries, Lord, and in Jesus' name, amenzzzzzzzzzz."

Hmmm. Sound familiar?

The Problem

There is probably nothing in the Christian life which is more advocated and less attempted, more urged and less understood or more praised and less practiced than prayer. That this should be so is a serious danger sign for our spiritual lives. But one more exhortation would probably not be helpful.

Part of the problem is that many sincere believers have really tried, time and time again, to pray—only to see their prayer lives drift into a listless routine because they simply have not found prayer to be the meaningful experience it is supposed to be.

Frequently we assume that dynamic and meaningful prayer should just come naturally, like talking to a good friend. When it does not, we become frustrated. But we do not think about the tremendous differences between prayer and human conversation. Despite the glib familiarity encouraged by some styles of evangelical piety, we do not really know God as well as we know our human friends and family; nor is the conversation taking place between equals. Jesus Himself encouraged us to think of Himself as our Friend and of God as our heavenly Father (John 15:14, Matthew 6:9). This intimacy, however, comes not as a natural condition, but as an unimaginable privilege, paid for by Christ's blood and affirmed by our obedience. (We are His friends in John 15:14 *if* we do what He commands.) The experience of this intimacy in its fullness is the outcome of a life of walking with the Lord, not something that can be expected to happen automatically. It is a privilege to be possessed, not a reward to be earned. Nevertheless, such experiences by their very nature cannot be entered into by the impatient.

The wonder of the Christian faith is that the One who is our heavenly Father is also the high King of heaven, the Lord and Creator of the universe, the great and awesome God whose thoughts are as far above ours as the heavens are above the earth (Isaiah 55:8-9). Yes, He cares for the fall of a sparrow, and yes, He loves us. Otherwise we would not dare to approach Him at all. But what does one say to a Being such as this? He invites us to bring Him our most trivial concerns, but surely a list of "gimmes" alone is a pitiful waste of our privilege. It is really not that great a wonder that we find ourselves getting tongue-tied and running out of things to say after only a few minutes. Maybe meaningful prayer is something that takes some growing into.

Then consider the fact that in human conversation we receive immediate, constant and objec-

tive feedback through the senses. I can watch my
companion's face, sense her body language, pick
up on her tone of voice, hear her words in immediate response to my own. I know at once how
she is responding to what I say or even whether
she is paying attention. Even then good communication is sometimes a challenge. But if I am in
any doubt as to whether I've been understood or
am understanding, I can always ask for clarifica-
tion.

But prayer is a very different proposition indeed. I have no sensory, objective, verifiable
means apart from the testimony of Scripture to
tell me whether God is even listening. Apart from
Scripture, I have no sure way of determining what
He is saying in response to my own words. I am
far from denying that the "still, small voice" of
God still speaks inwardly, but I must confess that
I often have a hard time distinguishing that voice
from the rationalizations and wish-fulfillment
dreams of my own wicked heart—again, unless I
check what it seems to be saying against Scripture.
But that involves *study*, and to believe that God
hears and cares and responds on the basis not of
feelings (which come and go) but of Scripture involves a continuous *exercise* of *faith*.

Prayer starts to sound an awful lot like *work!*
And lest this conclusion seem unspiritual, we
should remember some of the frequent biblical
phrases describing prayer: it is associated with
wrestling (Genesis 32:24), agonizing (Luke 22:44)
and groaning (Romans 8:26). We need not be dis-

couraged if prayer does not come easily. Apparently it is not supposed to.

In short, we need *instruction* in prayer. Good praying is not the simple thing it seems to be. Pursuing it raises a host of questions, both theoretical and practical. How do you talk to One whom you cannot see, whose facial expression you cannot observe, whose voice you cannot hear with the physical ear? What do you say to a Person who is omniscient, who knows your own thoughts and motives (the *real* ones!) better than you do? How do you approach this One who is *holy*, and who has the power to curse as well as to bless?

What can you say to a Person who loves you with a love as costly as Calvary, yet shows not the slightest disposition to pamper you and expects to enlist you as a soldier ready to sacrifice your all in the cosmic war of good and evil? How do we get started? What kind of language is appropriate? On what basis do we even *dare*?

The Solution

The disciples had the same questions that we do. They needed instruction too, and they asked for it: "Lord, teach us to pray" (Luke 11:1). Jesus' response to this request was rather interesting—indeed, unique, when you compare it to His normal way of answering questions. He did not answer their question with a question. He did not say, "Well, let Me tell you a story. A certain man . . ." He did not rebuke them for their lack of faith. For once, He gave a simple, plain and straightforward answer (11:2-4). He must have approved of their request. And if you are feeling the same frustration they did, He approves of yours as well, and would give you the same answer He gave to them.

The answer He gave was a model prayer His disciples could use. The prayer He gave in answer to the disciples' question in Luke is essentially the same as the fuller and more familiar version which appears in Matthew as part of the Sermon on the Mount (Matthew 6:9-13). We will use Matthew's version as the basis of our study, but we want to begin with the situation as described by Luke, for it highlights the fact that this is a prayer for disciples who want to pray better.

It was as Jesus was praying that a certain disciple was moved to make his request for instruction in prayer. We do not have any details about the prayer this disciple overheard, but we know that Jesus had been known to pray all night (Luke 6:12), and we have an extended sample of Jesus' own praying in John chapter 17. Something this man heard, at any rate, stirred in him a longing to be able to pray like Jesus. It was as a disciple—one who learns as an apprentice by imitating his master—that he framed his request, alluding to the fact that John the Baptist had taught *his* disciples to pray.

In this context, then, what Jesus would have given him was precisely a *model to follow*, a pattern to trace, a blueprint for Christlike praying. It was not then wrong for us to call it "The *Lord's* Prayer," though that designation is not scriptural, for its purpose is to help us learn to pray like Jesus; it represents the priorities and spirit of the Lord's own prayers. But it is even better to call it "The *Disciples'* Prayer," for it was provided for their use and adapted to their needs (Jesus Himself, for example, having no need to pray for forgiveness). Really, the great high priestly prayer of John 17 is more properly "The Lord's Prayer." This one is for us.

The Application

If it is a model or pattern, then, how are we intended to use it? I do not think it is wrong to recite it as a formula, but that use—which is almost the only one it now receives—was surely not the primary one the Lord had in mind. Surely the Master who warned against vain repetition (Matthew 6:7, KJV) did not stay up all night reciting this one paragraph over and over again! If that had been the case, the disciple would hardly have needed to ask; he would have picked up the formula already.

It makes much more sense to suppose that the prayer was given as an *outline* to follow. What Jesus was saying was, "This is how to approach God; this is how to address Him; these are the priorities you should have when you go to Him; and these are the things you should talk about. Take this prayer as a sample and an outline. Take these general petitions and make them personal and specific according to your own personality, needs and experience. That is how to pray

like I do." Nothing could be more practical, and
nothing could be more profound. It met the
needs of the first-century disciples, and it will
meet ours today as well.

As we study the various parts of the Disciples'
Prayer—the address, the individual petitions,
etc.—we will find it to be a powerful reshaper of
our priorities in both praying and living. It will
deepen our concept of who God is, and as we begin to enjoy the discipline of praying as our Lord
taught us, we will find ourselves knowing Him
better, loving Him more ardently and worshiping
Him more profoundly. It will enrich our experience of prayer because it will enrich our relationship with God. And the place to begin is to take
up the position of a disciple of Jesus, praying,
"Lord, teach us to pray."

Chapter 1

"Our Father"

What comes into our minds when we think about God is the most important thing about us.

— A.W. Tozer, *The Knowledge of the Holy*

"Hey, Dad, can I have the car keys? See ya!" And the son is gone before his dad can ask him about his day.

We sometimes take our human relationships for granted. Neither the father not the son may think about what it means to be a father or a son until it is too late. As a result, their relationship never develops the level of intimacy that is possible and that they both long for. These failed opportunities are nowhere more clear than in their attempts at communication. I wonder if the same thing happens between us and our heavenly Father? The way the Disciples' Prayer begins teaches us the importance of that relationship as the basis of prayer and its implications for the manner of prayer.

The Basis of Prayer

Before we can begin speaking to God, we must first know how to address Him, what kind of relationship we have with Him and on what basis that relationship rests. What makes us think that miserable creatures like ourselves, mites crawling around on a speck of dust orbiting an insignificant star on the outskirts of a nondescript galaxy, are worthy of His notice at all? Or what makes us think that, given the contempt we habitually manifest for His Word and His will, we really *want* Him to notice us? How dare we intrude our sinful natures and petty concerns on His holy and august presence? Until we have seriously faced questions like these, we are not yet ready to appreciate the privilege of prayer.

Without controversy, beings like us could only approach a being like God by invitation. Yet the incomprehensible good news which Scripture presents is that God has not only issued the invitation but stooped to solicitation: Jesus says that the Father actually *seeks* people like us to worship Him in spirit and in truth (John 4:23-24). And not only that, but the cross speaks of the inconceivable price He has paid to enable us to enter His presence without being annihilated. The whole gospel centers around His gracious attitude, His unmerited favor toward us. It is this gracious disposition on His part which makes prayer possible. So

Jesus gives a summation of every thread of this theme and raises it to its highest expression when He teaches us to address God as our *Father* in heaven. That God—in the light of our sins—is willing to let us remain as His *creatures* is grace beyond price; that He is willing to have us as His *servants* is a privilege beyond measure; that He authorizes us (and without His authorization we could not dare to do it) to approach Him as *sons* and *daughters* is a mystery of grace so great that no adequate response on our part is imaginable. We are simply overwhelmed in awe and wonder and worship.

The whole gospel is implied by the Lord's teaching us to call God our Father. For to address God as our Father is to confess that He can be approached only through the redemption which is in Jesus Christ. This is so because sonship for human beings in Scripture is always sonship by *adoption*. Why? Because ever since the rebellion of Adam, God has been related to the human race not as its Father but as its *Judge*. Our sins have necessarily caused an estrangement, a separation between us and God, with the result that we are cut off from Him. They specifically prevent Him from hearing our prayers (Isaiah 59:2). They cause us in our natural state to be not the children but the enemies of God, in need of reconciliation (Romans 5:10). The whole point of Christ's death was to satisfy God's justice by paying on our behalf the penalty of death which our sins demanded (6:23) so that the reconcili-

ation could take place without compromising
God's position as the upholder of cosmic righteousness (3:23-26). Christ's death purchases pardon for those who believe in Him, allowing them
to be restored to a relationship with God which
is not theirs apart from Christ. He is the way, the
truth and the life, and no one comes to the Father
except through Him (John 14:6). By virtue of
His death, He is the only mediator who can
bring God and man together on friendly terms
once again (1 Timothy 2:5).

The fatherhood of God is not something to be
taken for granted. The New Testament knows
nothing of the so-called universal fatherhood of
God and brotherhood of man. Apart from Christ,
God is not our Father but our Enemy and our
Judge, a position He reluctantly adopts in spite of
His love for us because of our sin, which His holiness cannot tolerate. Of those who do not believe,
Jesus said, "You belong to your father, the devil"
(John 8:44). But when we receive Christ as our
Lord and Savior and His death is applied to our account, our sins no longer stand in the way. God is
now free to relate to us once again, and the wonder
is that He chooses to do so as a father. Though we
were by nature His enemies, He *adopts* us as His
sons and daughters (Galatians 4:4-7). In ourselves
we have no right to expect anything from Him but
judgment; but when we receive Christ, He gives us
the right to be called His children (John 1:12).

When we pray to God as our Father in heaven,
we should be conscious of the fact that we are in-

voking an inestimable privilege, paid for by the blood of His only begotten Son, Jesus. Jesus is the only one who enjoys sonship as a birthright; the rest of us enjoy it by adoption. We ought by rights to be outcasts, but He has adopted us. And only those who have received Christ as personal Savior can claim this privilege. God is not your Father unless you have become His child through faith in Jesus Christ: unless, that is, you have come to believe that He is the Son of God who took on our humanity and died in our place and was raised from the dead by the Father, and you have by a definite act of the will chosen to confess your sinfulness, receive Him as your personal Savior and bow before Him as your Lord (Romans 10:9-10). These, and these alone, are given the right to say, "Our Father, who art in heaven." Those, in other words, who can pray "Our Father" are those who have already prayed, "God, have mercy on me, a sinner" (Luke 18:13).

To address God as our Father is then to be reminded of all we owe to God the Son. It is to identify ourselves as a people who have been bought with a price, and who consequently ought to glorify God in our bodies (1 Corinthians 6:20). It is to take our stand upon the ground of grace: "I stand upon *His* merit; I know no other stand, Not e'en where glory dwelleth in Immanuel's land." If we use our model prayer with understanding, then, we cannot pray without being reminded of the good news of the grace of God in Christ Jesus. This is a gospel prayer for gospel believers, and they alone have the right to appropriate its words as their own.

The Manner of Prayer: Attitude

Learning to address God as our Father in heaven not only implies the *basis* on which we approach Him, but it also has much to say about the *manner* in which we should approach Him. It suggests that we should come into His presence with an attitude combining love and respect—friendship and fear—intimacy and awe—warmth and wonder—confidence and quivering. He is our *Father* (hence the intimacy); but He is our Father *in heaven* (hence the awe). The phrase is comforting but not quite comfortable. It stretches us and takes us beyond ourselves even as we feel we are coming home.

Fatherhood itself is an image which combines the ideas of *care* and *authority*. A father is in the first place a person who has the responsibility to *provide* for his family. Jesus emphasizes this aspect in His teaching about God as Father. Because God is our Father we are not to worry about what we will eat or drink or wear. He feeds the birds and clothes the lilies, and we as His children are more dear to Him than they. Jesus does not discourage work and responsibility, but worry: our Father knows that we need these things (Matthew 6:25-32). "Which of you," Jesus asks us, "if his son asks for bread, will give him a stone? Or if he asks for a fish, will give him a snake? If you, then, though you are evil, know how to give good gifts to your children, how much more will your Father in heaven give good gifts to those who ask him!" (7:9-11). This fatherly concern and care is the basis of Paul's exhortation in Philippians 4:6-7: "Do not be anxious about anything, but in everything, by prayer and petition, with thanksgiving, present your requests to God. And the peace of God, which transcends understanding, will guard your hearts and your minds in Christ Jesus."

Since God is our Father we ought to approach Him in faith, with full confidence that He has our best interest at heart. He will not give us a stone instead of a loaf—and neither will He give us junk food, even if that is what we ask for, but rather good, wholesome homemade bread. He is a good Father. We can trust Him to be well-disposed toward our requests, and we can also trust Him to know when to say no. He is kind and loving, but not indulgent, for He is wise. He is everything a good and caring human father is, but without his faults and with his virtues magnified to infinity. He is our Father in heaven.

A father is also a person who has the responsibility to *lead* his family and to instruct and discipline his children. "Children, obey your parents in the Lord, for this is right" (Ephesians 6:1) and "Honor your father and your mother" (Exodus 20:12). Husbands and wives are, like all believers, to be mutually submissive to each other in the Lord (Ephesians 5:21); but within that mutual submission, the husband and father is given by God a special responsibility as leader of his family to which his wife should also submit (5:22-24). As head of his family, the husband/father is specifically to love and nourish it (5:25-29), a role which fits with what we have already seen of the father as provider above. But the use of the language of submission also clearly implies that a leadership role is in view, and this conclusion is consistent with biblical teaching about the father's responsibility in general.

We pray, in other words, to One who is not only a loving provider but also a loving *authority* concerned rather to train and discipline than to pamper us. God is not like the unloving human father who spares the rod (Proverbs 13:24), but rather He is our loving Father who deals with us as sons (Hebrews 12:5-11). Therefore we should receive gladly His discipline and instruction, take it seriously (12:5) and accept it like wise sons (Proverbs 13:1). Prayer, in other words, as a two-way conversation, involves our thoughtful response to God's *torah*, His loving fatherly instruction in Scripture. Profound praying is therefore the natural outflow of profound and obedient reading of the Word of God.

As our Father, God speaks to us in Scripture not just with good advice but with a father's authority, which commands our respect. Suppose I have asked my son to mow the grass. As his father and the head of our family, I have the authority to demand this of him and expect obedience. If he is negligent in carrying out my instructions, it will not destroy our relationship, though it may

put a strain on it if he is chronically and belliger-
ently so. But if he were to have cut the grass on
Saturday afternoon, imagine the conversation
which would ensue if on Saturday night he should
ask me for the car keys with the grass still uncut.
Even assuming that he has been merely negligent,
not rebelliously disobedient, it would take a bit of
nerve for him to come to me with his hand out for
the keys—more nerve, in fact, than I ever had
with my own earthly father, but no more, unfortunately, than we use with our heavenly Father all
the time.

Our relationship with God as expressed in
prayer is like that of a son or daughter to a good
father. We address God as children address their
father, not as they address a stranger on the one
hand or one of their buddies on the other. It is a
relationship of love, trust and intimacy—with a
good measure of respect and godly fear.

Even the relationship of a child to his or her
earthly father partakes to a large extent of these
characteristics, but the biblical analogy the Lord
gives us is qualified by an important modifier:
God is our Father who is in *heaven*, our heavenly
Father. If fatherhood in itself combines a basic intimacy with a certain amount of awe, the sacred
qualifier accentuates the awe. "The *heavens* declare
the *glory* of God" (Psalm 19:1, emphasis added);
we are reminded that the Father of whom we are
speaking is a Being capable of calling into existence and maintaining and controlling the whole
incomprehensibly immense and complex universe

of which our earth is an infinitesimal part. The
heavens—that inaccessible realm of light and
splendor—are merely the ripple of His robe as He
passes, an incomplete but eloquent hint of His
majesty and glory. Yet He is not some remote and
haughty potentate but One to whom we can cry,
"Abba! Father!"

Thus in one perfectly balanced phrase our Lord
brilliantly unfolds the richness of our relationship
to God. If we thought of Him merely as our Father, we would tend to take Him for granted as we
do our earthly fathers. If we thought of Him
merely as the Lord of heaven, we would be
abashed into silence before the intolerable weight
of His presence. But what He is to us is neither
one nor the other but the glorious combination of
both together: He is our *Father* who is in *heaven*,
not more, not less, not other. We hardly know
whether to climb up into His lap or fall on our
faces in the dust. There is unfortunately no physical gesture by which we can perform both of those
motions simultaneously. If there were, it would
perfectly express this attitude of the spirit. Thus
to know the meaning of this phrase in experience
is to know prayer as Jesus taught it to His disciples: prayer which is made to our Father who art
in heaven.

The Manner of Prayer: Language

The address to God as our Father in heaven has
implications not only for the state of mind that is
appropriate for prayer but for our language as

well. When we address One who is simultaneously the High King of heaven and our Father,
our language should be neither thoughtless on the
one hand nor formal on the other. He is neither
my fishing buddy nor a foreign dignitary; He is
my Father in heaven, and my language should reflect the quality of that relationship.

God of course is not impressed with our eloquence, and He will not be less prone to hear us
for our stuttering or bad grammar. Prayer is not a
performance on our part for an audience, divine or
human; it is communion with our heavenly Father. Being too self-conscious about our language
is a hindrance to good praying.

But with that warning in mind, it is still worthwhile to think for a moment about the language
we use. While Scripture requires no particular
style of speech for prayer, it does teach a particular frame of mind as appropriate, as we have been
seeing. And so intimately connected are our words
and our thoughts that bad habits in the one area
inevitably affect the other. When we lead others in
public prayer, inappropriate language can be a
stumbling block to their devotion, and insofar as it
discourages or subtly hinders the right frame of
mind, it can be a hindrance to our own as well.

For one thing, the Lord himself specifically for-
bade the use of "vain repetitions" (Matthew 6:7,
KJV). Unlike the heathen gods, our Father will
not be moved by many words. Sometimes using
no words at all is the best praying: "We do not
know what we ought to pray for, but the Spirit

himself intercedes for us with groans that words cannot express" (Romans 8:26). But whatever words we use—for in most cases we will use them, so verbally are our minds constituted—there is no virtue in multiplying or repeating them. There is nothing especially spiritual about long prayers just for their length.

Most of us probably do not spend enough time in prayer, but repeating ourselves is not the way to increase that time. Who, after all, are we trying to impress? We are speaking to our Father in heaven who knows what we need before we ask. That does not mean we should not ask; indeed, our need is exactly the reason we commune. But we do not have to supply the Omniscient with information, nor do we need to act as if He might not get the point, like a poor student, without our belaboring it.

How then *do* we increase the length of time we spend in prayer? We do it by broadening the range of subject matter which forms the context of our communion, which is precisely the point at which the Lord's outline is relevant, as we shall see.

Should we use *thee* and *thou*? Ironically, in the early modern English usage on which the King James Bible was based, these were *informal* forms, which contrasted with the more formal *you*, much as *tu* contrasts with *usted* in Spanish. People today who use King James language in their prayers generally do it because its antiquity makes it sound more formal and hence more reverent to them—the exact opposite to the effect these forms were originally intended to have! Not only that, but the Greek pronoun *sou*, translated "thy" in the KJV form of the prayer, does not even make the distinction between formal and informal like *thou/you* and *tu/usted*. So there is actually no direct authority in the original for either choice. The KJV translators had to choose, though, and they wisely chose the informal diction as more in keeping with the intimate nature of the prayer and with the Lord's own practice of using the informal and familiar Aramaic *abba*, which could be translated "Daddy." The cold and formal *you* would have been inappropriate to the father/child relationship as modeled by Jesus.

How do we apply this confusing welter of linguistic ironies today? The familiar or informal *thou* no longer communicates what it did for the men and women who used it as a natural part of their language. In fact, it communicates precisely the opposite. The KJV translators used it to avoid excessive formality; if we think they made the right choice, then the most faithful way of following their example in today's English would be to forgo its use ourselves. Perhaps in special situations in which extremely formal language is expected—say, the invocation or benediction at a graduation ceremony—such archaic language might be an option, if the speaker knows how to use it correctly. Or for eccentrics like myself who are, as it were, Elizabethans born out of due time, it might not be wholly unnatural. But for most people at most times there is nothing to be gained from the use of outmoded diction. Both the original Greek and the King James Version translators used what was the common, everyday language of the people of their time, whether the first century or 1611 A.D. If we are following the Lord's example, we will do likewise.

For most of us, there is no particular difficulty in avoiding excessive formality. But we must remember both sides of the balance. If formality is inappropriate in addressing our father, so thoughtless, slovenly, irreverent speech is inappropriate in addressing our Father in heaven. This problem becomes more obvious of course in public prayer, but many of the same habits carry over into our personal devotions as well.

I am, I confess, a bit troubled by the evangelical college student I once heard praising Jesus for being "such a bad dude" (which—I think—meant "a good man" in the slang of the time). I think his intentions were good, but the end result seemed, well, flippant. The tone of voice added something to the impression: I could imagine the fellow slapping the Lord on the back as he said it. Was this prayer symptomatic of a healthy spirituality, or had he traded a stuffy formality for something just as bad? I do not judge, but I wonder. Then there are the people who insert the word "God," "Father," "Lord," "Jesus," or even "uh" after every phrase. Perhaps in some cases it masks certain nervousness about praying in public. But it sounds so *unnatural*. My son does not talk to *me* that way. Would you want yours to talk that way to you?

Certainly one example of thoughtlessness in our prayers is the increasing tendency to address the Deity as "God" rather than "Lord" (which is better) or "Father" (which is what the Lord *said* to say). This is not the trivial issue it may appear to be. *God* refers to the type of being He is; *Lord* is His title or position. So to call Him "God" would be like my son addressing me as "man," and to call Him "Lord" would be rather like my son calling me "Professor Williams." (Note that "Lord" can be an appropriate form of address, for it also connotes a highly personal and theologically correct *relationship*, the relationship of a vassal to her liege.) Jesus knew what He was doing when He taught us that our normal way of addressing God should be as *Father*, for it is precisely this personal relationship which is the basis for the whole activity of Christian prayer. To call Him simply "God" is to substitute an abstract and impersonal concept for a concrete and highly personal relationship.

I am not suggesting that we should never call the Father our God or our Lord: these words impart important truths which we may and should express to Him in prayer. But what I am picking up on as I listen to people praying these days is a dramatic shift in habitual address from the concrete to the abstract. The whole rich range of vocabulary is reduced to only one term; it is the most abstract and least personal in connotation of

the lot; and it is *not* the one the Lord Himself in-
structed us to use as our habitual and most natural form of address. This trend indicates an
impoverishment of our concept of God which
can lead only to an impoverishment of our spirituality—eventually sapping the Church's spiritual vigor.

One of the most significant ministries we can
have today is to help reverse this trend by our
own example when we have the opportunity to
lead in public prayer. The normative biblical pattern for prayer is that it is made to the Father in
the name of the Son with the aid of the Spirit. To
lose this rich biblical framework and replace it
with a simplified abstraction is to weaken the
whole Trinitarian foundation of the Christian
faith. We do so at our peril.

Because prayer is made to our Father in heaven,
we should not become so self-conscious of our
speech or afraid of using the wrong words that we
cannot speak freely to Him. Rather, we should try
to avoid the extremes of excessive formality on the
one hand or thoughtless irreverence on the other.
We should remember, and our prayers should reflect, the Trinitarian foundation on which the
whole structure of Christian prayer is erected.
Within this framework, whatever language is
natural for you does not call undue attention to itself and is both sincerely affectionate and sincerely
respectful and reverent is ideal. The key is simply
to pray as our Lord taught us: to our Father who
is in heaven.

The Manner of Prayer: Submission

To pray to God as our Father in heaven is to approach Him through the redemption which is in Christ Jesus and with a combination of love and respect, intimacy and awe, reflected in the very language we use. It is also to remember that we approach Him as a *Person*, and an exalted one at that. This point would seem too obvious to be made if we did not so frequently hear people bringing their requests to God as if He were some kind of cosmic vending machine. We think that if we just insert enough coins of faith or works or promises into the slot, the desired blessing will automatically drop out. But we are not dealing with a mechanism; we are dealing with our heavenly Father. He is a Person with His own wisdom, His own will and His own agenda. Consequently, prayer never has results which are quite predictable—fortunately for us. We may get what we ask for; we may get it in a form or at a time we did not envision; or the answer may be, for our own good or His greater glory, simply "No."

Of course, as we are dealing with a Person rather than a vending machine, there is much more to prayer than making and receiving requests. But even on the level of asking and receiving, it is much more fun to pray to our heavenly Father than to a predictable blessing dispenser. He is faithful to His promises, but He is also full of surprises. In every way it is His creative personality which allows for what we can only call the romance and the adventure of prayer.

God is a much better father than I am, and the gap between His knowledge and wisdom and my own is infinitely greater than that between mine and my children's. Nevertheless, it was when I became a father myself that I really began to appreciate what it means to have God as my Father. Some of the frustrations I thought I had with His way of dealing with me evaporated, and I developed a sort of sympathy for His position I had never imagined before. If my greater experience of the world leads me sometimes to frustrate my children's short-term expectations for their greater good in the long run, or for other reasons they are simply not in a position to comprehend, how much more often must the heavenly Father deal with me in exactly the same way!

A few years back when my children were small, we took a short vacation trip to St. Simons Island on the Georgia coast. Between unpacking and going out for dinner, I took them swimming in the motel swimming pool. After about an hour, I made them get out—something they were not ready to do by a long shot. But I knew that at that stage a longer stay would have resulted in sunburn. So, as a loving father I disappointed them— and Heather said, "You're mean!" But I wasn't—and neither is God when He does the same kind of thing. Then the next morning they wanted to get back in the pool, but I said, "No, this time we're going to the beach." They had had such a good time in the pool that they took this announcement as another disappointment and thought Dad was the most unreasonable person on earth. But you should have seen their eyes when they saw the ocean for the first time! All was forgiven—or, more accurately, their com-plaints were forgotten, swallowed up in the greater joy of what I had planned for them.

The point is that if God is a *Father* to us, we must expect to find the same kinds of experiences in our relationship to Him that my children fre-quently have with me—only more so. And prayer is one of the focal points of that relationship where this is true. We pray to a Father who is also an in-finitely creative *Person* who is infinitely wiser than we; and we have it on his authority that

No eye has seen,
    no ear has heard,
no mind has conceived
    what God has prepared for those who
        love him.
        (1 Corinthians 2:9)

But sometimes our stubborn insistence on our own way keeps us from getting to the beach—or being able to enjoy it when we do. The essence of the whole relationship is learning to *trust* Him. That is why so-called "unanswered prayer" is sometimes the prelude to His greatest gifts, if only we trust Him. And that is why prayer is such an adventure: It is the focal point of a relationship which is the greatest adventure man has ever known.

Summary

The first step to deepening our prayer lives is to remember to whom we are praying: our Father who is in heaven. He is the One we approach by the great privilege of adoption through the re-demption which is in Jesus Christ. He is the One we approach with a unique combination of love and respect, intimacy and awe, as One who cares for us but who is also in an exalted position of authority over us. He is the One we approach as a Person with His own wisdom and agenda. If we understand why the Lord began His model prayer as He did, then we may truly pray, "Our Father, who art in heaven—hallowed be thy name."

Chapter 2

"Hallowed Be Thy Name"

Blessed be the God of Heaven and Earth!
Who only doth wondrous things.
Awake, therefore, my Lute and my Viol!
Awake all my powers to glorify thee!
      —George Herbert, *The Country Parson*

Gratias agimus tibi propter magnam gloriam
      tuum,
we give thee thanks for thy great glory.
      The *Gloria in Excelsis*

"You scared?"

"What, are you kidding? Of course I'm scared. Who wouldn't be? You heard what these guys did in their last battle. Their God—what was His name?—is great, and He fights for them. If the big boys couldn't beat them, what chance do we have?"

"I know. But they'll kill us anyway, so we

might as well take a few of them with us! Sell your life dearly, brother."

"Ready! Here they come! Aieee!"

"Take that, you swine! I can't believe it—they're running. Come on, men! I guess their God isn't so great after all."

It was a dark day in the history of Israel. Achan the son of Carmi had taken for himself a beautiful mantle, 200 shekels of silver and 50 shekels of gold from the spoils of Jericho—all which had been placed under the ban and devoted to destruction by Jehovah. Because of this sin in the camp, the armies of Israel, though fresh from their dramatic defeat of the mighty city of Jericho, had been put shamefully to flight by the puny little two-bit village of Ai.

> Then Joshua tore his clothes and fell face-down to the ground before the ark of the LORD, remaining there till evening. The elders of Israel did the same, and sprinkled dust on their heads. And Joshua said, "Ah, Sovereign LORD, why did you ever bring this people across the Jordan to deliver us into the hands of the Amorites to destroy us? . . . O Lord, what can I say, now that Israel has been routed by its enemies? The Canaanites and the other people of the country will hear about this and they will surround us and wipe out our name from the earth. *What then will you do for your own great name?* (Joshua 7:6-9, italics added)

The Meaning of "Hallow"

"What then will you do for your own great name?" I think Joshua would have understood the first petition of the Disciples' Prayer, and I also think he would have understood why it was first. Joshua was concerned about the present situation, and he was concerned about the future of his people. But he showed his deepest concern when he expressed those concerns in terms of a concern for the glory of God.

It is no accident that Joshua's greater Namesake would give as the first petition of His model prayer, "Hallowed be thy name": May Your name (in other words) be holy. It is an amazing request, when you stop to think about it, like asking for a circle to be round or a square to have four sides. God's name is *intrinsically* holy. Nothing we do could in the slightest way add to or detract from that holiness, which ever dwells in self-sufficient splendor and unapproachable light.

But Jesus was not recommending idle or meaningless words as the staples of our praying; these therefore must represent a real request. What they must mean is something like this: May Your name be *recognized* as holy, *treated* as holy and *reverenced* as holy. This beginning petition in fact flows logically from the address: If we really understand who it is we are praying to, if we really know what it means to pray to our Father in heaven, then "Hallowed be thy name" will *have* to be the first thing on our minds when we approach Him.

A Biblical Pattern

This logic exemplifies a pattern engraved deep upon the pages of Scripture and most evident at the crucial high points of God's self-revelation. The Ten Commandments, that great Old Testament summary of His moral character and consequent demands on us, show the pattern clearly. The Ten Commandments are traditionally divided into the "Two Tables" of the Law. Whether or not the commandments actually broke down thus on the two original tablets of stone, there is a logical progression in their order. The first group deals with our relationship to God: do not have other gods, do not worship idols, do not take the Lord's name in vain, remember the Sabbath to keep it holy. The second group then turns to our relationship with other human beings: honor your parents; don't murder your neighbor, commit adultery with his wife, steal his possessions, lie about him behind his back or even covet what is his. On the basis of the vertical we square up the horizontal. We must relate rightly both to God and man, but God comes first.

When we see the Ten Commandments in this light, we recognize that Jesus' great summary of the law is precisely that: it summarizes the Decalogue perfectly.

> "Love the Lord your God with all your heart and with all your soul and with all your mind." This is the first and greatest

commandment. And the second is like it: "Love your neighbor as yourself." All the Law and the Prophets hang on these two commandments. (Matthew 22:37-40)

Jesus, in other words, picked out of the Old Testament two verses—Deuteronomy 6:5 and Leviticus 19:18—which in their new context summarize and focus the Ten Commandments for us as the Law of Love. The First Commandment sums up the First Table of the Law, which now becomes a manual for loving God; and the Second Commandment reveals the Second Table as a handbook for loving our fellowman. Jesus' Law of Love is not a replacement for the Old Testament Law, but quite literally a summary of it which constitutes at the same time a brilliant commentary on its true meaning. And it picks up and reinforces the original pattern: We begin with the vertical and then move to the horizontal. God's glory comes first and is the foundation on which we build the rest.

The Lord's principle of priorities in Matthew 6:33 shows us the pattern again: "Seek first *his* kingdom and his righteousness, and all these things will be given to you as well." God is indeed the Lord of all of life, so if we do indeed relate properly to Him in the context of His will as revealed in the total scope of Scripture, then everything else can be rightly expected to fall into place. If He does not occupy the first place, then all of life is thereby skewed. We are right to be concerned about temporal things—the temporal world is, after all, the one in which we were created to serve. But the way to take care of them is to begin with the eternal: Seek *His* kingdom *first*, do not be anxious about things like food and clothing, and the God who feeds the sparrows and clothes the lilies will give these other things to us as well.

Lest we think this perspective occurs only in the Law and the Gospels, the apostle Paul gives a pretty good statement of it in the epistles too: "Whether you eat or drink or whatever you do, do it all for the glory of God" (1 Corinthians 10:31). Paul makes even more clear the relationship between the two dimensions. Precisely because the vertical perspective comes first, it gives light to everything in the horizontal plane, and that illumination is the basis of their ultimate unity. It is in mundane things like eating and drinking—indeed whatever we do—that God is to be glorified, as we "work out" the salvation He has worked in us (Philippians 2:12). But the vertical/eternal/divine and the horizontal/temporal/human only mesh properly when God and His glory come first in our thoughts, our work and our prayers.

It is not then surprising that the prayer Jesus gave His disciples as a blueprint for their praying fits the pattern. Here as in these other texts the imprint of the same divine Mind is clearly seen. Just as in the Ten Commandments, we begin with the vertical: may *His* name be hallowed, may *His* kingdom come, may *His* will be done. Then a second group of petitions deals with our needs: give us *our* daily bread, forgive *our* sins, deliver *us* from evil. The pattern is too consistent to be accidental. There is a spiritual logic to the organization, the very outline as well as the substance of the prayer. It resonates with the Decalogue—and especially with Matthew 6:33—like the ringing of a thousand church bells. Seek first His kingdom (mentioned specifically in both passages) and other things (like daily bread, prominent in both contexts) will be added. If repetition serves for emphasis, nothing in the Bible is emphasized more than this.

The Priorities of Prayer

Before we even look at the particulars of prayer, then, its general organization sets a radical agenda for our priorities. In general, the glory of God is to be the first thing on our minds when we pray; in particular, the sacredness of His name. I am afraid, though, that our actual prayers betray all too often an insufficient reckoning with these lessons. Be honest. What is the first thing *you* typically think of to say? Robert Murray McCheyne said, "What a man is on his knees before God, that he is—and nothing more." Ouch! It follows that a primary reason so many believers lack the full measure of joy, power for service and victory which faith in such a great God ought to give them (1 John 5:4) is that their very *prayers* reveal them to be focused not on the Father at all, but on themselves. Perhaps the greatest service the Lord performed in giving us this prayer was to remind us that the first concern of heart, mind and soul as we approach the throne of God is not to be our daily bread, not deliverance from evil, not even forgiveness of sin—it is to be, "What then will You do for Your own great name?"

Precisely because the logic of prayer is reflected as much by the organization as by the substance of the Disciples' Prayer, using it as an outline for our praying allows it to function as the molder of our priorities as it was meant to be. We should use it as an instrument to that end. Every time we pray we will be reminded of what is truly important. We will begin with "Hallowed be thy name." If this order does not come naturally to us, then we can make it deliberate, using the Lord's outline to focus our priorities until the right order *is* second nature to us.

Letting the prayer the Lord gave us set the agenda, we take each petition and expand it by making it personal and particular as we meditate on its meaning for us. With this first petition the process might go something like this: "Hallowed be Thy name. May Your name be set apart, honored, revered and respected as holy—by me and by others. *By me*: is there anything in my life which would dishonor rather than glorify it? As You point these things out to me, I confess them, repent of them and ask Your help in overcoming them. *By others*: I am grieved when I hear Your name being taken in vain, when people do not re spect You in general. How may I live so that my association with You will inspire others to reverence You as I do?"

We can continue making the prayer more specific, in terms of particular individuals or situations about which we are concerned. Obviously different people will be led in different directions from this point of departure; but this place and no other is the place to begin, as we express to God— and by expressing reinforce and deepen—our concern for His glory: "What then will you do for your own great name?"

It is essential that when we arise from our place of prayer we put our money where our mouths have been—and our time and effort too. Christlike living should flow from Christlike praying, and then become the context out of which that Christlike praying continues with increasing sincerity, focus and intensity. And this cycle should continue, spiraling ever upward to glory. If it does not, then our praying was not Christlike at all, whether based on His model or not. We are nothing but hypocrites.

Prayer and Praise

To hallow God's name is to begin by refocusing our priorities; it is also to begin with *praise*. We begin with a concern for the glory of God and the honor due His name. And as we speak to Him of this, we also naturally go on to ascribe that glory to Him even as we pray. If we are not moved to ascribe all honor, glory and majesty to His name,

we have not yet understood what it means to pray
to our Father who is in heaven.

Praise is made an essential element of prayer
not only by the nature of the One to whom we
pray, but by our own nature as well. Deep-seated
in every human being is a natural impulse to give
voice to his or her admiration of whatever reveals
itself as excellent. I remember hiking in the
Rockies with a friend of mine a few years ago.
We kept looking at the massive, snow-covered
peaks and the majestic vistas all around us and
saying over and over again, "Isn't this *great*?" It
was an involuntary response; it was not very ar-
ticulate, but *something* was demanded by our surroundings. To have suppressed it would have
required a major effort. The response is sometimes wrung from us even when we do try to
suppress it.

Just sit in a major-league baseball stadium. The
hometown fans may boo the opposing players at
every opportunity; but let one of them make an
Ozzie Smith acrobatic catch deep in the hole at
short and while still off balance somehow throw a
perfect strike to first, and the boos will (at least
momentarily) turn to oohs and ahs, in spite of the
fact that the results are bad for the good guys. To
withhold praise from that to which it is due is contrary to our natures, though we have perverted
them to the point that it is possible to do. But it
goes against the grain of what we were made to
be. The enjoyment of any good thing is not complete until that thing is *praised*, and until the praise

has been rendered we are left feeling empty and unfulfilled. If it was *really* good we may feel impelled to talk of nothing else for weeks.

We feel this way because giving praise is what we were created for and redeemed for. As the Westminster divines put it, our "chief end" is to "glorify God and enjoy Him forever." For this purpose we were created, from this purpose we fell and to this purpose we are restored by salvation. In the first chapter of Ephesians, Paul summarizes all God has done to achieve our redemption: election, predestination, redemption, revelation, sealing, etc. Three times he breaks into his list to emphasize and reemphasize the purpose behind it all: it is "to the praise of his glorious grace" . . . "for the praise of his glory" . . . "to the praise of his glory" (Ephesians 1:6, 12, 14).

All the other things we praise are just a warm-up to this purpose and should in fact be a subsidiary part of it, for He deserves our praise above all and is in fact the Creator and Source of all else that is praiseworthy. We are meant to do it before others, and we are meant to do it before Him. It is the ultimate fulfillment of our natures; it is our destiny. If we have truly known Him—to the extent that we truly know Him—we will find it natural, indeed irresistible, an impulse welling up spontaneously and involuntarily from within, to praise Him.

But what if, in spite of our best intentions, our praise still seems cold, forced and perfunctory? Scripture is full of practical help for those who find themselves in such a state as one of the tragic results of sin. The first step is to remember that praise *is* our reason for being and our destiny. Meditate often on those passages of Scripture which speak of the greatness of God and of our salvation and calling until you recapture once again the excitement of the vision George Herbert expressed so well:

> Of all the creatures both in sea and land
> Only to Man thou hast made known thy
> > ways,
> And put the pen alone into his hand,
> And made him secretary of thy praise.

The book of Ephesians makes an excellent study in this regard.

Second, we must put away all unconfessed sin. Psalm 24 sandwiches the following question and answer between two passages of unsurpassed praise:

> Who may ascend the hill of the LORD?
> > Who may stand in his holy place?
> He who has clean hands and a pure heart,
> > who does not lift up his soul to an idol
> > or swear by what is false.
> He will receive blessing from the LORD.
> > (24:3-5)

With these issues resolved, there follows the joyous shout for the gates and the everlasting doors to lift up their heads so the King of Glory can come in. Sin is the canker which blights the plant of faith before it can yield the fruit of praise; it is the weight which holds us captive to earth when our souls would rise up into the courts of heaven; it is the house of mirrors which makes the beauty of the Father's face seem grotesque and hideous to us. To free your praise, confess your sins, for "he is faithful and just and will forgive us our sins and purify us from all unrighteousness" (1 John 1:9). The free pardon purchased for us by the blood of Christ is both one of the greatest occasions for our praise and the great enabler of it as well.

Finally, we should make use of the many examples and patterns of praise God Himself has given us. God deserves the best praise we can give Him. Richard Baxter exhorts us to "Conceive of this duty of praising God according to its superlative excellency as being the highest service that the tongue of men or angels can perform."[1] When we praise God, we join our voices not only with the angel choirs but also with those of all the saints throughout history—and they have left us some powerful examples to follow. One of the best ways of enriching our own praise is to make use of the rich legacy of praise which the saints of old have left to the Church in their hymns, poems and prayers.

The evangelical tradition in America has been suspicious of "set" prayers. We value spontaneity and confuse it with sincerity. We are afraid of "go-

ing through the motions," but we often end up repeating our own shallow and banal phrases rather
than someone else's profound and moving ones.
These are legitimate concerns, and I am far from
advocating an abandonment of spontaneous
prayer. But we have allowed these fears to cut us
off from our inheritance and thereby to impover-
ish our worship unnecessarily.

There is no necessary reason why praying in
someone else's words must be insincere,
unauthentic or not heartfelt. Most of us in fact
pray in other people's words every week, when
the pastor or others "lead" us in prayer during
public worship. Why not let Augustine, Luther,
Calvin, George Herbert, John Donne, Charles
Wesley, John Newton, Isaac Watts or Gerard
Manley Hopkins lead us in prayer? Most believers
are utterly ignorant of the great body of profound
but understandable devotional poetry which came
out of the great age of classical Protestant orthodoxy in the seventeenth century; they have never
heard of George Herbert, the greatest devotional
poet of all time. They forget how many of the
great hymns of Wesley, Cowper, Newton and
Watts are theologically deep and biblically based
prayers of praise to God.

A good place to start is simply praying through
the hymnbook, even if we cannot sing. The soul
will sing in praise to the Father who was praised
so well by men of old. Wesley's "And Can It Be
That I Should Gain?" is a good place to begin. Really think through what Wesley was saying to

God in that hymn, and then say it along with him. If you are not praising God for His "amazing love" with greater understanding and consequently greater fervor by the end, you are a walking corpse! These hymns remind us that theology which does not lead to doxology is unworthy of the God we serve.

Most importantly, follow the patterns of praise God has given us in Scripture. Baxter exhorts us again: "Read much those Scriptures which speak of the praises of God; especially the Psalms: and furnish your memories with store of those holy expressions of the excellencies of God which he himself hath taught you in his word."[2] These words are profound and accurate, focused on God as He really is. They give us simultaneously the subject matter for our praise and a divinely sanctioned model for its style. We can safely and securely appropriate these words as our own, mold our hearts into the shape they define and offer them up to Jehovah as an acceptable sacrifice indeed. As we memorize these words, they also come to us to deepen and enrich our own thoughts when we are praying spontaneously in our own phrases. In every way, the most important path to meaningful praise is to saturate ourselves with Scripture.

With the Bible in our hands, we need never be tongue-tied in God's presence again. Do you lack eloquence to praise the Lord as He deserves? Open your Bible, and you can pray with the passionate lyricism of David, the sweet Singer of Is-

rael. Open your Bible, and you can pray with the
profound and majestic phrases of Isaiah, the
Prince of Prophets. Open your Bible, and you can
pray with the unique combination of theological
precision and missionary zeal of Paul, Apostle Ex-
traordinaire. Open your Bible, and you—who are
a clod of dust, by nature a sinner and unworthy to
come into God's presence at all apart from the
Blood—can pray with the elegant, pure and powerful simplicity of Jesus Christ.

Summary

What would such praying sound like? We
would find ourselves crying out with Joshua,
"What then will you do for your own great
name?" We would find ourselves shouting with
the Psalmist,

> Not to us, O LORD, not to us
>   but to your name be the glory,
>   because of your love and faithfulness.
>   (115:1)

We would find ourselves with Paul praying to
the Father of glory that we would grasp, with all
the saints, the breadth and length and height and
depth of the love of Christ and be filled with all
the fullness of God in the One who makes known
His name among the nations (Ephesians 3:18-19).
And we would find ourselves praying like Jesus
that God might glorify His name in us (John 17).
And these are only isolated examples of what we

would find ourselves desiring if Scripture indeed set the agenda for our prayers.

"What then will you do for your own great name?" This is the place at which Jesus would have us begin. It is what He wants to be the first thing on our minds when we pray. If we would be men and women of prayer, we must first become children of God through faith in Jesus Christ and thus be able to say, "Our Father." Then we must begin with the sacredness of His name. And if we hope to hallow it rightly, we must begin with Scripture, especially the Psalms. We must read it, meditate upon it and feed our souls on it until it fills them to overflowing. Then we will truly be able to pray as our Lord taught us: "Our Father, who art in heaven . . . hallowed be thy name."

Notes

1 Richard Baxter, *The Christian Directory*, vol. 1 of *The Practical Works of Richard Baxter*, 4 vol. (London: George Virtue, 1838), 147.

2 Ibid., 150.

Chapter 3

"Thy Kingdom Come"

Jesus shall reign where'er the sun
Does his successive journeys run;
His kingdom stretch from shore to shore,
'til moons shall wax and wane no more.
　　　　　　—Isaac Watts, *Hymns, Songs, and Poems*

Thou art coming to a King;
Large petitions with thee bring.
For His grace and power are such,
None can ever ask too much.
　　　　　　— John Newton, *Olney Hymns*

"What are we supposed to do?" The knight muttered, shaking his head so that the bedraggled plume on his helmet flopped pitifully back and forth. "The merciless heathen roams the land at will; our people are starved, murdered or enslaved. And we are powerless to stop it. What kingdom is this? We have no kingdom!"

"True," Merlin agreed. "We have no kingdom because as yet we have no king. But the sword is still there in the stone, and someday the one for whom it is reserved will come and pull it out. Then when the king comes, the kingdom will come. Where the king is, there the kingdom will be. As strong as the king is, so strong will the kingdom be. They will sing songs about us, my friend, for when *that* king comes, we shall have a kingdom indeed—and then we shall have peace."

"Whoever you are," the knight said fervently, "I've got one thing to say: thy kingdom come!"

*   *   *

There is perhaps no passage of Scripture which has more to teach us in such short compass about God, our relationship to Him and the whole Christian life than this passage we traditionally call The Lord's Prayer. We have already seen how it teaches us to approach God as our heavenly Father by adoption and how it requires us to come to Him as people chiefly concerned with the honor, glory and praise due to His name. We begin with God before we move to our own needs; and beginning with God, we start with the glory of His name and move on to the performance of His will: "Thy kingdom come."

The Reign of God

The Greek idiom "kingdom of" means something like "rule or reign of." When Jesus proclaimed that the kingdom of heaven was "at hand," He meant that God was about to assert His authority over the earth; He was about to break into history in a decisive way to accomplish His purpose and work His will. The reign of God was about to begin, or at least enter into a new phase. And that is exactly what happened: Jesus defeated Satan at the cross in such a way that God could reign as King once again in the hearts of people who had previously been rebels and outlaws. In receiving Christ as Lord by faith, they received forgiveness for their prior treason and restoration to citizenship under their true and rightful King. Forsaking their former allegiance to Satan the Usurper, they are restored to fellowship with God on the basis of the work of Christ—and the kingdom comes.

To pray "Thy kingdom come" is to say something like this: "May You rule—may You reign—may You be sovereign in my life, in the Church and in the world. I bow to Your Lordship and desire to serve You as Your loyal subject; command me, and I will obey!" It is very close in meaning to the next petition: "Thy will be done." In fact, the two are really twins, partners in the typical Hebrew parallelism of the Old Testament poetic literature. Their closeness in meaning makes them mutual commentaries one upon the other, while their differences in connotation bring out insights which would be hidden were they not yoked together. So we are also saying we want God's will to be done: "May all who seek to do Your will be strengthened, and those who rebel against it be thwarted in their evil designs." This, of course, we make specific according to the issues relevant to our times and situation. "So work in me that I may understand and desire Your will as I ought and pursue it above all." All this is implied by the two petitions taken together.

If we are correct in seeing these two petitions as an example of Hebrew poetic parallelism, then they are in one sense a single petition. But the embellishment, the repetition, makes this petition stand out with special emphasis; most of the others do not receive this treatment. "Hallowed be thy name" receives special emphasis by being first; "Thy kingdom come / Thy will be done" receives it by being repeated. We will reflect that stress in our study by giving a separate chapter to each half of the parallel.

The point to be noted first from that emphasis is this: in our prayers, our study of Scripture and our living, there is to be an *active concern with the will of God*. The thrust of our praying should not be, "Give me, forgive me, protect me, and, oh, if there is an order I'll consider it." Rather, an early and heavy priority in our praying is to be the expression to God and cultivation before Him of an active, sincere and fervent desire for Him to show us His will that we may do it. This means that prayer as a conversation with the Father flows out of a context of serious study of the Bible as the source, not primarily of *blessings*, but of *marching orders*. (The blessings tend to come when they are not our primary focus anyway.) In other words, we are to pray, "Thy kingdom come."

The notion of the kingdom of God is a rich concept in Scripture, and the Lord by including it in our model prayer suggests that it is a concept which should enrich our praying, specifically as we seek God's will. It is worthwhile then to ponder what it is we are really praying for when we pray for the kingdom. In what sense does God reign or rule when we see around us a world intent on thumbing its nose at His authority in every area of life? Exactly how does—and when will—the kingdom come? In what sense did it "come" with Jesus, and how will His second "coming" affect the status of the kingdom? Biblical answers to these questions will help us pray the second petition more intelligently.

There are at least three different aspects of God's reign over the cosmos which are relevant to our prayers: we might speak of them as the three "kingdoms" over which He rules. Of course these three are really one kingdom, as the Father, Son and Spirit are one God. Our God reigns—period! But it is still helpful to analyze that rule into these three aspects or phases to help assure a full understanding of it on our part.

The Providential Kingdom

First is what we might call *the providential kingdom*, or the rule of His Providence. This refers to God's control of the forces of nature, circumstances, etc., guiding history to the goal He has planned for it. Scripture is full of references to this aspect of the kingdom. God guides the stars in their paths (Job 38:31-33, Psalm 8:3, 147:4); He sets bounds for the ocean which it cannot pass (Job 38:8-11); He numbers the very hairs of our heads (Matthew 10:30); and not even a sparrow can fall off a branch without His consent (10:29). Through all the circumstances of time and history, He rules and overrules to work all things together toward a predetermined end which is good for those who love Him (Romans 8:28). Though evil is allowed a certain scope of operation as the price for human freedom, God remains in control. Nothing happens without His permission, and the outcome of history is never in doubt. He exercises this control through the providential kingdom.

Perhaps the best summary of God's rule from this perspective is Ephesians 1:10, which also relates it specifically to the history of salvation. Ephesians 1 is a summary of all God has done to achieve His eternal purpose of bringing glory to His Son through the salvation of sinners. Election, predestination, redemption, revelation—all this has been done "with a view to an administration suitable to the fulness of the times, that is, the summing up of all things in Christ" (Ephesians 1:10, NASB).

The word translated "administration" is *oikonomia*, which can mean economy, dispensation, stewardship, administration or management. "Times" is *aion*, literally "ages"; the phrase "fulness of the times" is an idiom referring to the com-

pletion of a series—in this case, the completion of
the progression of ages. "Summing up" is a highly
technical Greek word, *anakephalaiosasthai*, used by
Greek rhetoricians to refer to that moment of a
discourse when everything that is being said is
brought together—the point from which the unity
of the whole and the relationship of each part to
that unity is clearly seen. Today, we would call it
the "thesis statement." What Paul is saying is that
when time has run its course, it will be revealed
that God has been so managing the course of history behind the scenes that Jesus Christ will be revealed as the ultimate meaning of the universe.
Everything is moving inexorably to that one final
summation because of God's stewardship of His
creation, His management or administration of all
things. That is His rule in the kingdom of His
Providence.

But how do we make the providential kingdom
a matter of prayer? God will maintain control of
things in any case. We can hardly ask for the
providential kingdom to *come*—it is already here.
But we can make the wonder of this mystery a
topic of meditation before Him and praise Him
for the way it manifests His glory. We can realize
that His sovereignty over the cosmos is the foundation for the other aspects of His reign which
have not yet come to full fruition in our experience, and we long for that time. To say, "Thy
kingdom come" at this point is to say, "We are
glad that You rule providentially; we affirm that
rule and thank You for it." We can then make the

prayer more specific in terms of our own experience of His providence in all its marvelous detail.

God indeed deserves great praise for His providential care and protection of us. From the way in
which the planet was prepared as a hospitable
habitation for us—just the right distance from the
sun, etc. (Isaiah 45:18)—to the unique details of
our own history, there are marvels here enough to
support a lifetime of meditation.

My dad was a pretty good private pilot, and
when I was a boy we used to do quite a lot of flying together. One day we were on our way to visit
a friend of his, planning to land our Taylorcraft in
his cow pasture—a maneuver we had successfully
performed on a number of occasions. But this time
was to be different. We were banking in over the
treetops just above stall speed, ready to drop into
the clearing which was visible just ahead, when
the plane was caught in one of those summer dust
devils, a miniature whirlwind. Only this one had
not picked up any dust and so was invisible. We
were spun around like a top. When it left us, we
had lost all our airspeed and pancaked right down
into the trees. Two saplings caught us in our de-
scent, one under each wing. The wings bent back
and the saplings bent down, absorbing most of the
energy of our impact, and we came to rest sus-
pended in the trees a few feet from the ground.
Just inches from the nose of the plane was a massive, solid oak which would have smashed us to
bits had we gone straight into it. As it was, we
walked away with only a few cuts and bruises.

Who was it that planted those two saplings at precisely the right location to save us, planning for our accident two decades before it occurred and before I had even been born? Was it chance that dictated that, of all of the seeds released into the air, those two at that time just happened to fall in the right location and take root and thrive? Statistical probability proves nothing, for all events are equally improbable if indeed the universe is ruled by chance. But my knowledge of my heavenly Father tells me that it was an instance of His rule in the providential kingdom, one which by its dramatic nature happened to catch my attention. Each of my readers can think of his own stories, and all of them together are just the tip of the iceberg of what we owe to God's providential care. Because they are the visible part, they should serve to remind us to thank and praise Him for the rest.

The Kingdom of Grace

A second aspect of God's rule, and one which was probably more in the forefront of Jesus' mind when He announced that the kingdom of heaven was at hand, is what we might call the gracious kingdom, or *the kingdom of grace*. This refers to Jesus reigning as Lord in the hearts of believers through the Word and the indwelling Holy Spirit. In this sense the kingdom "comes" to an individual when he receives Christ as his personal Savior. All people are subject to God's rule in the providential kingdom, but they are subjects in rebellion. Believers are those who have been pardoned for their rebellion and restored to citizenship; they then are privileged to experience the rule of King Jesus not only providentially but also graciously and personally. Because of the sacrifice and mediation of Christ, God ceases to be their Judge and becomes instead their Father and their good and gracious Lord. Together they make up the true Church as those whose citizenship is in heaven (Philippians 3:20, Hebrews 11:13-16).

The visible church always has weeds among the wheat, and it is a mistake to *identify* it with the kingdom; but it is the primary way in which the kingdom of grace manifests itself on earth. We are here as ambassadors of our true country, emissaries of the rightful King whose rule has been restored in us and one day will be restored over all (2 Corinthians 5:20; Philippians 2:10). We are empowered as the ambassadors of this kingdom to offer the same free pardon we have received. All who confess their treason and forsake it, swearing allegiance to the true King, will receive it and be restored to citizenship with us. Those who refuse that allegiance will be compelled to submit as traitors and outcasts. The King *will* reassert His rule. It can be embraced or it can be imposed, but come it will, and in believers it has begun to come already. Meanwhile, He graciously postpones the time of imposition to give us opportunity for embracing His pardon and His Lordship so that we may receive Him back with joy.

This perspective on salvation has implications for how we view the so-called "lordship salvation" controversy. Those who accuse the advocates of "lordship salvation" of teaching salvation by works have profoundly missed the point. The question is not whether salvation can be had on any other basis than grace alone. *Nobody* deserves the pardon, and there is no question of anybody receiving it as a reward for meritorious service. It is offered as an extension of pure grace, unmerited favor, on the part of the King. The question is whether a rebel can be restored to citizenship without recognizing the claims of the rightful King and swearing fealty to Him. How can he receive the pardon unless he recognizes the authority of the King to grant it? And this recognition of necessity entails a reaffirmation of allegiance. Until that happens, he is still a rebel, and as such must be executed for high treason. To lay down one's arms and publicly acknowledge the legitimacy of Christ's kingship—to confess Him as Lord, as Paul puts it (Romans 10:9-10)—is not so much an arbitrary condition of receiving the pardon as it is a logically necessary part of the *act* of receiving it. This does not mean Christ's new subject will be a perfect one; but unless he confesses Him as his Lord he cannot claim Him as his Savior. To do so is utterly contradictory both to logic and Scripture.

So the kingdom comes when the King comes, and it comes to us when we receive Him as personal Savior. What happens when a new and good king comes to the throne of an evil and corrupt kingdom? Reform happens. The old, wicked counselors are removed from office and replaced by loyal and righteous men of integrity. The old, evil laws and customs are reformed, to the ultimate benefit of all the subjects and the glory of the king.

The same thing happens to us when we become a part of Christ's gracious kingdom. Old things pass away, and all becomes new. The influence of humans and their banal media and degraded philosophies is replaced by the whole counsel of God in Scripture; the old, self-centered lifestyle is replaced by new wholesome and godly pursuits. The process of reformation is not complete in a day, but if it has not begun, then no change of administration has taken place either, and we are yet in our sins (1 Corinthians 6:9-11). The King cannot come without reforming the kingdom over which He reigns, and that is why the call to repentance was part of the gospel of the kingdom: *"Repent,* for the kingdom of heaven is near" (Matthew 3:2, Mark 1:15, etc., emphasis added).

When we pray, "Thy kingdom come," we are saying at least three things with reference to the kingdom of grace.

Praying for world evangelization

First, we pray for world evangelization: may the kingdom come to people in general (especially to the people being ministered to by the missionaries we have committed to pray for), to So-and-So, the friend I am witnessing to or to Thus-and-Such, my unsaved loved one. As we pray for these people, we can ask the Lord to bring to our minds specific things we can do to further the answer to our prayers: a note to write, a call to make, an answer to an objection to be given at the next opportunity. We can bring the specific names, needs and hindrances to the advancement of the gospel that our missionaries have mentioned in their prayer letters before the Lord, dwelling on each for a moment. We can also let the fact sink in that our missionaries are God's primary means of extending His kingdom around the world—and we are the primary means of extending it in our neighborhoods. So as the Lord through His model prayer teaches us to pray, "Thy kingdom come," He is teaching us to be missionary-minded people. To pray the Disciples' Prayer with understanding then is to advance His kingdom both by unleashing His power for its work and by deepening our own commitment to the kingdom's mandate, the Great Commission.

Praying for the Church

Second, and because of this, our prayers for the Church, its spiritual health, its mission, its pastors and its missionaries fit here. May the world, we ask, be able to see the difference the King makes among His own people, and may it thereby be attracted to Him as He receives glory in the Church. To pray for the coming of the kingdom is to ask not only that more people accept the true King as their own, but also that He become more fully, intimately and effectively present in the lives of those who are already His. If we really want the kingdom of grace to come, we will pray for our own pastor and elders, missionaries, Sunday school teachers, youth workers and lay people by name. Why? Because God has ordained to advance His kingdom through them or not at all. And He can only advance it *through* them if He advances it *in* them. Where the King reigns, there is the kingdom; where He reigns unopposed in power, there is peace.

Praying for ourselves

Finally, we are concerned for the advancement of the kingdom in our lives: May God's grace in the person of His Son increasingly come to rule every aspect of our being for our own good and His glory. In all three of these areas we want the kingdom increasingly to come. It will not come in its fullness until the King returns; but it has come and is coming. We live in the age of the Foretaste, the Pledge and the Deposit (Ephesians 1:14), and we long for the full inheritance ultimately and for a fuller installment even now. So we pray, "Thy kingdom come."

The Kingdom of Glory

That longing leads to the consideration of the third aspect of the kingdom: *the kingdom of glory*. The kingdom comes when the King comes, and it will come in its fullness when Christ returns to rule over the earth. The glorious kingdom is the fulfillment and consummation of all that we see in the providential reign of God and in the gracious reign of Christ. The external control of providence and the internal triumph of grace will be united in one eternal, unbreakable and glorious kingdom in which the Father has put all things under the feet of the Son, and Christ is all in all (1 Corinthians 15:24-28).

Many believers divide the kingdom of glory into two further phases: *the millennial kingdom*, a literal 1,000-year reign of Christ upon the earth (Revelation 20:4-6), and *the eternal kingdom*, in the new heavens and earth which follow the millennium. But all true Christians agree on one thing— they long to see their Lord face-to-face, and so they pray, "Thy kingdom come." Whatever our view of the details of prophecy, we who serve as the King's ambassadors long for the return of the King.

But how can we logically pray for the coming of the kingdom in this final sense? Jesus was quite clear that the times and epochs have already been "fixed" by the Father's authority (Acts 1:7), and the Father already knows the very day and hour (Matthew 24:36). If there is any way to bring that time closer, it would be not by prayer but by evangelism (24:14). But of course, evangelism is it-self something we should be praying for, and it is in fact a part of this petition with respect to the kingdom of grace, as we have seen. But we also can and should be praying for the coming of the kingdom of glory more directly.

We should pray "Thy kingdom come" in the first place, because it should be our greatest desire to *see* the King face-to-face, and this desire needs to be expressed.

I was once away from home for a week as a delegate to my denomination's national conference. A couple of times during the week I called home to touch base and make sure everything was going fine. And during one of these conversations, one of the kids said to me, "Daddy, we miss you. Hurry home!"

Now, in fact this was a request I could not fulfill. The day and hour of my return had already been set by Delta Airlines, and there was business which had to transpire first. So it did not fit into the larger plan for me to say "Yes" to my daughter's petition. But do you think that it did not matter to me whether or not she asked? Heather's request did not alter the time of my homecoming, but it did enrich the quality of the experience for both of us when it did happen. It also made a difference in our relationship during the waiting period in the meantime. So once again Jesus' choice of the father/child analogy as the theological basis for prayer turns out to be perfect. We need to be looking forward to our Lord's return, and, like my daughter did with me, we need to tell Him so.

The second coming of Christ should be an event in which we have a vital interest, and this interest should find expression in our prayers. It will mean the final defeat of sin and the final healing of all its effects: death, sorrow, suffering, sickness,

pain, loneliness, boredom, futility and meaning-
lessness. It will mean the final triumph of the rule
of God which has already begun in the kingdom
of grace: "We know that . . . we shall be like him,
for we shall see him as he is" (1 John 3:2). It will
mean the completion of Christ's bride and His
body, the Church—gathered from every tongue,
tribe and nation, the last elect sinner foreknown
from before the foundations of the earth believing
and saved. It will mean the final fulfillment of all
the promises of God, which we experience par-
tially as pledge and down payment here and now.
The second coming is an event we have a great
stake in indeed.

But while we show an obsessive fascination for
the guessing game we play with the details of
prophecy, our spiritual forebears would probably
see in us a lack of personal longing for the Lord's
appearing which would seem to them a symptom
of spiritual shallowness. Praying the second petition of the Disciples' Prayer with understanding is
one way of combating that shallowness, one
which is prescribed by the great Physician of our
souls Himself.

The effects of so praying are a deepening of our
relationship with the Lord and also an increase in
our zeal for evangelism. When we learn to pray
any of these petitions from the heart, we will find
ourselves putting our money where our mouths
are when we get up from our knees. And evangelism is the primary way we have of directly has-
tening the coming of the kingdom and the King.

The kingdom comes to individuals as they believe the gospel, and how shall they hear without a preacher? And it will not come in its fullness until the gospel has gone forth to the ends of the earth and some of every tongue, tribe and nation are included (Matthew 24:14). Personal soul winning and support of missions are the primary ways we show our sincerity when we pray "Thy kingdom come." And praying "Thy kingdom come" is the primary way we make our evangelism and support of missions effective. Neither can really thrive without the other.

Summary

It is, in short, not possible to live the Christian life, fulfill God's purposes for us or please the Father without praying consistently, earnestly, fervently and with understanding the second petition of the Disciples' Prayer: "Thy kingdom come." In other words, "We are glad that You rule; we praise You for the way You rule; may You rule us more fully; may Your rule be consummated in every way." In providence, in grace and in glory, He is the King of kings and Lord of lords, and He shall reign forever and ever. Amen.

Chapter 4

"Thy Will Be Done"

We cannot be safe, much less happy, except in proportion as we are weaned from our own wills and made simply desirous of being directed by His guidance.

— John Newton, *Letters*

"What is God's will for my life? Should I be a pastor, a missionary, a teacher or a businessperson? Should I trust God to keep my old 'bomb' running or trust Him to help me make the payments on a new car? I really like Joe. Maybe we're in love! But how do I know if this is the one God wants me to marry? And how can I ever be *sure* I'm not missing God's best for my life?"

As a college professor and a pastor, I hear a lot of questions like those. It is encouraging to know that young people truly care about the will of God for their lives, though sometimes in their search for the big picture they can be found neglecting the obvious and simple statements of His will found in the Bible. Maybe they would get a clearer idea of whether the Lord wants them to be career missionaries if they were already being witnesses to the people across the street.

There is another set of questions which might not sound like they are related to the first set, but really are. "I've prayed all semester about my school bill. All my friends have had 'mailbox miracles,' but now I've either got to take out a loan or leave school. Why doesn't God care about me?" Or "Look at all the suffering in the world: Abortion kills one-third of all babies in the womb, half of all marriages end in divorce, and I've got close friends who were abused as children and can't get over it. Why doesn't God *do* something?"

In all these things we are praying for God's will, sometimes wrestling and agonizing before Him concerning His will. His will is a simple thing in itself, but it can surely become complex when applied to the twisted messes which are our daily lives. Nevertheless, understanding the theology that underlies Jesus' instructions for us to pray about God's will can go a long way toward helping us comprehend the heart of the Father and the adventure which is the Christian life.

In one sense, the second and third petitions of the Disciples' Prayer are really one request, repeated for emphasis using Hebrew synonymous parallelism. If the Greek idiom "kingdom of" means "rule or reign of," as we have suggested, then "Thy kingdom come" means "May You rule;

may the sovereignty You have by right be exercised fully and made manifest in my life, in the Church and in history." The next petition, "Thy will be done," is implied by and included in that request. But in addition to repeating it for emphasis, it also nuances it for our fuller understanding: It focuses it on a specific aspect of God's rule. One very important effect of Christ's taking the throne of my life in the kingdom of grace should be for God's will to be carried out in and through me. One effect of Christ's taking the throne of the universe in the kingdom of glory will be that His will is carried out on earth as it is in heaven.

Prayer and the Will of God

Effective prayer is rooted in an understanding of who God is. So we begin by addressing Him as our Father in heaven and by reminding ourselves that His name is holy and should be hallowed. Moreover, we do not fully reckon with who God is until we reckon with His *sovereignty*: We pray for His kingdom to come. And if we worship a God who is sovereign, it follows that effective prayer will be prayer that is focused on the will of God. Acceptance of Christ as Lord and Savior is obviously a prerequisite of such praying. Until the issue of salvation has been addressed, we are not His subjects at all, but rebels against His kingdom and enemies to His cause, whether consciously or not. Once the issue of who is the rightful king has been settled—once we have made the great confession of the early Church: *kurios christos*, "Jesus

Christ is Lord"—then our prayers can begin in earnest. Because we believe in Him as Lord, we want His will to be carried out, and we want to be His instruments to that end. So we pray, "Thy will be done."

Prayer that is focused on the will of God will be effective prayer, both in terms of communion with the Father and in terms of receiving positive responses to our requests. As our wills become more in tune with His, we will less often make requests which His goodness and wisdom lead Him to deny. As we learn more of His will from Scripture and begin to pray in accordance with the will of God, we will find our priorities changing. In our prayers we seek to align our priorities with His. As we learn more about His priorities from His Word, we express them back to Him as our own, and by thus expressing we reinforce these lessons of Scripture.

Scripture indeed has much to say about the relationship between our priorities and our prayers. The most basic principle of priorities is found of course in Matthew 6:33: "But seek first his kingdom and his righteousness, and all these things will be given to you as well." "These things" in context are material things like food and clothing—things which the next petition will authorize as matters to pray about. Right priorities are a condition of the promise that they will be given. In fact, we will discover that in every way proper priorities are a prerequisite to effective prayer.

James has an interesting application of the Lord's principle: wrong priorities can be a reason for "unanswered" prayer. "When you ask, you do not receive, because you ask with wrong motives, that you may spend what you get on your pleasures" (James 4:3). Selfish prayers are not necessarily answered affirmatively. God likes pleasure, as Screwtape reminds us: He invented all of them, and the devil is reduced to perverting those God has made or tempting people to take them in the wrong way or at the wrong time. The whole infernal research department has never been able to produce a new pleasure of its own. Pleasure is God's province, and He wants to give it to us— but not when pleasure, rather than His will, is the thing we are after.

David had the right perspective: "You have made known to me the path of life; you will fill me with joy in your presence, with eternal pleasures at your right hand" (Psalm 16:11). There is no lasting pleasure to be found apart from God. Once again, those who seek His kingdom first will have everything else thrown in. Those with other priorities get left out—not because God is stingy, but because they are looking for the wrong things in the wrong places.

The Psalms are a treasure trove of wisdom which can help us ground our prayers in the will of God. "How great is your goodness, which you have stored up for those who *fear* you" (31:19, emphasis added). "The lions may grow weak and hungry, but those who *seek* the LORD lack no good thing" (34:10, emphasis added). "Cast your cares on the LORD and he will sustain you; he will never let the *righteous* fall" (55:22, emphasis added). To *fear* the Lord is to reverence Him as God; to *seek* Him is to value your relationship with Him above all else; the *righteous* are those whose sins are covered by the blood of Christ, believers who have confessed Him as Lord.

Those, in other words, who are rightly related to the Father are the ones who are in touch with His kindness and who experience the benefits of being His children. The primary function of prayer then is to experience that relationship as we seek Him ("Our Father . . .") and fear Him ("Hallowed be thy name"). We know that we truly seek Him and fear Him when the cry of our hearts is, "Thy kingdom come; thy will be done." As Jesus put it Himself, "If you love me, you will obey what I command" (John 14:15, cf. 14:21, 23).

The connection Jesus draws between love and obedience cannot be overemphasized. The Christian life is neither a form of legalism nor is it antinomian. A system of rules is not our focus, but we want to do His will simply because it is *His* will: We love Him because He first loved us. Asaph asks, "Whom have I in heaven but you? And earth has nothing I desire besides you. . . . It is good to be near God" (Psalm 73:25, 28). He was seeking first the kingdom of heaven—in the person of the King. Thus he would have agreed with David's philosophy of prayer: "Delight yourself in the LORD and he will give you the desires of your heart" (37:4). If God, His Word, His will and His ways are indeed our delight, the desires of our hearts will be for things He delights to give. The purpose of prayer is first to cultivate, express and reinforce the state of mind Jesus and the psalmists were describing and modeling as we enter into communion with the Father. Then—and only then—it is to ask and to receive.

Effective prayer is focused on the will of God as a part of being enamored with the person of God. It follows that it is also *submissive* to the will of God. The submission flows gladly and naturally from the focus. Here our great Example is, of course, the Lord Jesus Christ Himself. In the last hours before He had to face the cross, everything about Him shrunk from the burden of sin He was about to bear. It is impossible for us to imagine what this prospect must have meant to Him: He who had from all eternity enjoyed perfect fellowship with the Father was about to become in the Father's eyes all the ugliness, filth and corruption of the accumulated sin of the human race throughout all of time in order that we might be released from that burden (2 Corinthians 5:21). And, despite His love for us, the idea of being identified with *sin* was all but intolerable to His holy consciousness. So He told the Father exactly how He felt about it: "My Father, if it is possible, may this cup be taken from me" (Matthew 26:39). But His prayer did not end there. "Yet not as I will, but as you will."

Something got the Lord up on that cross in spite of His abhorrence at being identified with sin. What was it? His love for us was a factor, no doubt; on this Scripture is quite clear (John 3:16, 13:1, 15:13, etc.). But what was foremost in His mind as He prayed, what He actually expressed at the critical moment, was His commitment not to us but to the Father: "not my will but yours." What actually got Jesus through the crisis was a lifetime of praying as He had taught us to pray: "Thy will be done."

Those who pray like Jesus did here are prepared in advance to accept a possible "No" or "Yes, but later" or "Yes, but not as you envisioned it" as the answer to their prayers. It was not in fact possible for the cup of God's wrath against sin to pass from Jesus, not if mankind were to be redeemed. His prayer did not gain Him release from the trial, but by reconfirming His commitment to doing the Father's will it did help Him find the strength to face it. And so it frequently is for us. Wise people *want* God's answer to their prayers to be "No" sometimes; to feel otherwise is to feel that we are wiser than He is. And if the thing we pray for is more important to us than God's will, we are guilty of idolatry: We are worshiping the gift instead of the Giver. Thus, "Thy will be done" is not only an individual request in its own right, but it is also the foundation on which *all* our petitions are erected. In right-minded praying, the kind that Jesus modeled, it is a provision attached to everything we ask: "if it be Your will."

This perspective helps to explain the troublesome and confusing "blank checks" the Scripture seems to give us when we pray. A number of passages taken at first glance seem to say that if we have enough faith, we can get whatever we ask for. "Ask and it will be given to you; seek and you will find; knock and the door will be opened to you. For everyone who asks receives" (Matthew 7:7-8). "If two of you on earth agree about anything you ask for, it will be done for you by my Father in heaven" (18:19). "If you believe, you will receive whatever you ask for in prayer" (21:22). "Therefore I tell you, whatever you ask for in prayer, believe that you have received it, and it will be yours" (Mark 11:24). "I will do whatever you ask in my name" (John 14:13).

These passages are problematic because nobody has ever had the experience of automatically getting everything he asked for—*not even Jesus*, as we have seen, or the apostle Paul (2 Corinthians 12:8-9). Did these people fail to work up enough faith or neglect to get another believer to "agree" with the request? In the case of Christ, at least, this would be inconceivable. Not only that, but the blank check these passages seem to hand us is contrary to the wisdom Scripture teaches elsewhere. James 4:13-16 teaches us to qualify our plans and intentions with "if it is the Lord's will . . ." (4:15), recognizing that God's plans may not coincide with our own. Would this principle not apply equally to our prayers?

The "blank check" interpretation of these passages conflicts with experience, reason and Scripture, and it leads the saints to blasphemous prayers and testimonies. Whatever Jesus might have meant by these sayings, it could not have been anything that would have encouraged us to treat God as anything less than God.

What then are we to make of these promises? I would suggest that they make most sense when seen in the light of their total context in the whole scriptural doctrine of prayer. They presuppose the Creator-creature relationship, the Master-servant relationship and the Father-child relationship as the context in which they are to be understood. They are prayers in the name of Jesus and prayers of faith in Jesus, who is our Lord. Faith in God means trusting Him with our whole lives, and it implies submission to His will. So all these prayers are assumed to be in that context: They are prayers such as the ones we saw modeled in the Psalms and in the whole life of Jesus—which includes Gethsemane.

The passages are not then blank checks for immature Christians to cash in for whatever selfish, shortsighted and petty objects they desire. They are descriptions of what prayer can be like for people who have learned to pray like Jesus, people who have learned to trust the Father to know what is right and to do it. Prayers in which we arrogantly dictate to God or try to manipulate Him are not prayers of faith at all, and the promises do not apply to them. We cannot manipulate God by trying to get up enough subjective certainty that He will do what we want; that is not ultimately *trust*. The prayer of faith is prayer that is made according to the will of God as it is revealed in the totality of Scripture. There the principle has already been laid down that when we delight ourselves in the *Lord* we will receive the desires of our hearts (Old Testament) and that when we seek His kingdom and will *first* everything else will be given (New Testament). The seemingly absolute promises are made to people who are assumed to have already mastered the earlier lesson—people who pray, "*Thy* will be done."

Guidance and the Will of God

While the "first table" of the prayer is focused on God rather than our needs, there is one personal need which fits logically under this request: our prayers for guidance. When we ask for guidance, we want to know God's will for our lives in general or for a situation in particular. And, of course, we can only expect Him to reveal His will to us if we are prepared to do it (John 7:17). James tells us that guidance should be a matter we pray about: Those who lack wisdom should ask for it, unwavering in their faith commitment, and it will be given (James 1:5-8). The Father may respond to such requests in many ways: through providence (the "opening" or "closing" of doors), the counsel of pastors or mature Christian friends, etc. But the primary way He responds is through the Bible.

"*Your Word* is a lamp to my feet and a light for my path," says the psalmist (Psalm 119:105, emphasis added). "How can a young man keep his way pure? By living according to your word"

(119:9). Paul tells us that Scripture is adequate for all the exigencies of life: "All Scripture is God-breathed and is useful for teaching, rebuking, correcting and training in righteousness, so that the man of God may be thoroughly equipped for *every* good work" (2 Timothy 3:16-17, emphasis added). We are told both that the way to light our path is by the light of God's Word, and that this light will be sufficient for the task.

This does not mean, of course, that we can find which car to buy, whom to marry or what college to attend or job offer to accept listed in a complete concordance. But it does mean that the whole counsel of God gives us all the principles we need to discern the will of God in the totality of life. Applying those principles takes wisdom, which God promises to supply. But the place to begin in any decision is not looking for iffy, subjective inward impressions but rather looking for the biblical teachings which apply to the problem.

If (a big if) we have mastered and are following all the biblical principles and commandments which apply to a given situation, then we may do as we please, confident that we are thereby doing the will of God. This confidence and this freedom come from taking seriously Paul's statement that Scripture is adequate for every good work. Prayers for guidance then are first and foremost prayers for a fuller understanding of Scripture.

We must know the will of God if we are to do it. "Thy will be done" then reminds us that prayer is a two-way conversation, and that we can be sure we are hearing God's half of it clearly when we correctly understand what the Bible says. Christ-like prayer is not just a list of "gimmes." It is our personal response to what God says to us in Scripture. And at the very heart of that response should be a heartfelt, "Thy will be done."

On Earth As It Is in Heaven

We should be concerned not only with God's will for us, but also for His will in the world around us ("on *earth* as it is in heaven"). And this concern also should find expression in our prayers. Though God has the authority and the power to impose absolute obedience on all people at any moment, He has graciously postponed that imposition of His rule so that the free offer of pardon under the kingdom of grace can be extended to humanity. Thus, in His "forbearance," He continues to "pass over" most of the sins we commit (Romans 3:25).

In other words, until the time for the kingdom of glory arrives, He *permits* a number of things to occur which are not in accordance with His will considered absolutely. Because He wills to give us further opportunity for a free response to the gospel—opportunity to embrace His rule by choice rather than by force—He logically must also allow for His will to be rejected on a short-term basis. Hence, until Christ returns, we must distinguish between His absolute will and His permissive will. (God's "absolute" will we could call His "simple" will: what He desires but does not neces-

sarily decree—for example, that all people should
be saved. His "permissive" will would be what He
allows to happen, even though it is contrary to His
will on a deeper level—for example, that people be
permitted to sin or reject Him. He never wills sin
directly, in other words, but He does will that human choices have significance. Hence He indi-
rectly "wills" that sin be permitted.) He is not
willing that any should perish, but that all should
come to repentance (2 Peter 3:9); but neither is He
willing that any should be saved *apart from* repentance and faith in Christ.

The existence of evil—actions and events which
are in one sense contrary to God's will—is necessary at this time for the sake of His higher purposes. Nevertheless, the existence of evil is
grievous to Him, and it should be to us as well.
Anything which is contrary to God's will is hurt-
ful to His creatures, in the long run, as well as
painful to Him. And He does not accept this necessity stoically and passively. Though the time is
not yet appropriate for Him to eradicate all opposition to His will by an act of irresistible super-
natural force, He still opposes such evil through
the ministry of His saints in moral persuasion and
loving, sacrificial service. He also may intervene to
judge evil or redeem its effects through direct su-
pernatural action, in limited ways which are in
keeping with His general plan for this age of the
world. His deliverance of Israel from bondage or
of Lot from the destruction of Sodom and Gomor-
rah would be examples of such action.

The point is that God intervenes to overthrow the opposition to His will (sin) for the sake of His people and in response to their prayers. The exodus was set in motion when God heard the cries of Israel (Exodus 2:24-25), and Abraham's intercession would have saved the whole city of Sodom from destruction if only a few more righteous people could have been found (Genesis 18:32).

God could end the spiritual warfare which rages on our planet immediately if He chose to do so, but He allows it to continue so that more individuals may have the opportunity to come to Christ. When the last saint has been saved, it will be over. But until then, part of our responsibility is to minimize the cost of allowing it to continue. We do so by acting as salt and light in a corrupt society (Matthew 5:13-16). We promote conformity to God's ideal by example and by persuasion, and doing so has a soteriological—saving—as well as a temporal function: As we show the peaceable fruit of righteousness, the harmony and well-being that conformity to God's will brings, not only do we make things better but people see our good works and are led to glorify our Father who is in heaven (5:16). The healing which our obedience promotes gives credibility to our preaching of the gospel. And that our preaching and witness should have such credibility is definitely one thing we should seek from God in our prayers.

In sum, it should bother us when God's will is not done, and we should rejoice when it is. We should therefore work to oppose evil and promote righteousness, and we should therefore pray for God's blessing on that work. We should pray against the workers of iniquity and for those who oppose it and try to bring about healing. Surely it is not God's will for unborn babies to be murdered freely, for standards of decency to be trampled into oblivion, for the marriage bond even of believers no longer to be held sacred. If He permits these things to the extent that He does, part of the reason may be our own sloth. If we value His will as we ought, we will work and we will pray about these issues and others like them. God may intervene supernaturally in response to our prayers; He will give us wisdom and strength to do His will. But if we are not asking, we do not yet understand what it means to pray as Jesus taught us, "Thy will be done."

Summary

One-half of the model prayer our Lord gave us is concerned with God rather than our own needs—the *first* half. We pray, as the expression of our whole lives, to desire, seek and praise God for His glory and His will. So until the purposes of God are more important to us than our petitions, the law of God more important than our lusts and the will of God more important than our wishes, we have not yet begun to pray like Jesus.

When God's will *is* more important and we *have* begun to pray like Jesus, we will be ready to discover that the Father is very concerned with our personal needs and desires. Indeed, the first and deepest one, though at first we probably were not aware of it as such, was to learn to put Him first. One function of the Disciples' Prayer is to teach us that lesson, which it does by modeling the ordering of our priorities in its very structure. It starts with God's person, His name, His kingdom and His will, but it does not stop there. The same prayer which takes us into the rarefied mountain air of God's eternal purposes for us is also full of the down-home aroma of freshly baked bread. It is equally appropriate in the throne room of heaven, in the marketplace of life and around the kitchen table.

But that is another chapter.

Chapter 5

"Our Daily Bread"

Oh Lord, refresh our sensibilities. Give us this day our daily taste. Restore to us soups that spoons will not sink in, and sauces which are never the same twice. Raise up among us stews with more gravy than we have bread to blot it with and casseroles that put starch and substance into our limp modernity. . . . Above all, give us grace to live as true men—to fast until we come to a refreshed sense of what we have and then to dine gratefully on what comes to hand. . . . Deliver us from the fear of calories and the bondage of nutrition; and set us free once more in our own land, where we shall serve thee as thou hast blessed us—with the dew of heaven, the fatness of the earth, and plenty of corn and wine. Amen.

—Robert Capon, *The Supper of the Lamb*

We had just moved to a new city to pursue the academic training required for the ministry to which the Lord had called us. We had been promised a job and a place to live, but it was becoming evident that the people who had made those promises could not be trusted. We had a station wagon crammed with all our earthly possessions, which included no money and no income. Classes at the seminary were starting in two days. What could we do?

Three years later the scenario repeated itself. We had managed to leave seminary with no debts, but no money either. It was another new city and a doctoral program, and the apartment a well-meaning friend had arranged for us was filthy and infested—utterly unlivable. Apartments and utilities all required advance deposits, summer jobs were scarce and wouldn't provide checks for several weeks even if found immediately. We were down to the last jar of peanut butter. What could we do?

What we could do—the only thing we could do—was to depend on the Lord. And He responded in ways that amazed us. A friend dropped by out of the blue with a $20 bill: "The Lord told me to give you this." I found a job doing inventory at a local store that (unheard of!) paid in cash at the end of each day. What we did on these occasions, and others like them, was to receive a crash course in the practical meaning of the next petition in the Disciples' Prayer: "Give us this day our daily bread."

What we have already learned about prayer, God, life, ourselves and the whole Christian faith from our study of the Disciples' Prayer could be enough to occupy us for a lifetime. We have seen that we can approach God as our heavenly Father by adoption through the redemption which is by faith in Jesus Christ. We have learned that we are to come into His gates with singing and into His courts with praise, the glory and sanctity of His name being our first and primary concern. We have realized how the Disciples' Prayer can be a powerful instrument for reordering our priorities, giving us an active concern with the will of God. We have discovered that the three "me's" of prayer (give me, forgive me and help me) are not to be our primary focus in praying or living.

Now we are ready to learn that these concerns *are* to be a *part* of our focus because they are necessarily a part of our lives as we serve the Lord. But we enter into them and pursue them in the context of, in the light of and for the sake of the concerns in the "first table" of the prayer. And the first of these temporal needs which our Savior invites us to address is the need for our daily bread.

The Relevance of Bread

Perhaps the first question which the text raises is why this, out of all our temporal needs and concerns, should come first? Once we turn to our own personal needs, why should not the prayer for forgiveness receive the position of preeminence? The forgiveness of sin is certainly the most critical need that fallen people have, and in one sense it is the prerequisite to all praying. We cannot have fellowship with God until the barrier of sin has been removed by the blood of Christ, and we cannot enjoy that fellowship until confession and repentance have consciously brought our renewed transgressions under the blood, claiming the promise of First John 1:9. Thus it is logically necessary that the life of prayer in general and every prayer in particular begin with "God, have mercy on me, a sinner" (Luke 18:13). How can anything—especially something so trivial as our daily bread—come before that?

The answer is that nothing can—but that did not happen to be the point that the Lord was trying to make on this occasion. The Bible in general and Christ's ministry in particular give ample emphasis to the centrality of the cross. The simple fact that Passion Week occupies as much space in the Gospels as the rest of the Lord's earthly life put together is only one indication of this truth. Perhaps the fact that the prayer was a model for disciples rather than for sinners seeking salvation gave Jesus the opportunity to make another important point: the primacy of God's glory in prayer and the Christian life. And indeed, we do find the need for forgiveness literally central, right in the middle of the portion of the prayer devoted to our own felt needs. In addition, the prayer has other ways of stressing the importance of forgiveness. By beginning with God's holiness and will, it reminds us of how far short we fall of both. By addressing Him as Father, it reminds us of His grace as the ground of our relationship.

Still, it is striking that the prayer for our daily bread, ostensibly the most mundane and least "spiritual" of the requests in the second part, comes ahead of the others for forgiveness of sin and victory in spiritual warfare. It is almost as if the Lord wanted to reassure us that, in the midst of the exalted spiritual atmosphere of much of the prayer, the most mundane details of our lives are legitimate concerns of our praying. It seems to emphasize the fact that, as the Bible views things, there is no distinction between the realms of the "sacred" and the "secular." *All* parts of creation were made by God and will be redeemed by God (Romans 8:18-22). *"Every* good and perfect gift is from above" (James 1:17, emphasis added) and is clean if it is received with thanksgiving (1 Timothy 4:4). Paul sums up the biblical attitude well: "So whether you eat or drink or whatever you do, do it all for the glory of God" (1 Corinthians 10:31).

The God who gave us bodies which need nourishment also gave us bodies that enjoy it, and He means them to. Appreciating His good gifts, recognizing them *as* His gifts and helping others to enjoy them too is one way of giving glory to His name. In God's eyes, it is no less spiritual to fix lunch than to prepare a sermon. A sour asceticism which demeans the physical dimension of life is simply spiritual ingratitude, as evil in its own way as the idolatry of gluttony. God opposes indulgence, but not enjoyment. (Rightly understood, the two are not ultimately compatible anyway.) So do not be too "spiritual" to pray about your daily bread, lest you be found in the highly dubious position of thinking yourself more spiritual than Jesus.

The Meaning of Bread

What then exactly do we ask for when we pray for our daily bread—literally, "loaf"? The Lord here employs a figure of speech known as "synecdoche," a figure in which the part stands for the whole. A rancher uses it when he refers to 300 "head" of cattle; he means 300 whole cows, not just the heads. The part stands for the whole. Bread then represents not just bread but food in general.

I can't help thinking of the routine on TV's *Hee Haw* in which Grandpa Jones is asked what's for supper. He always replies with a short poem scientifically designed to make your mouth water. So here, with apologies to Grandpa Jones, is my "expanded paraphrase" of this petition:

> Fried chicken, good and hot,
> Green beans (with fatback in the pot),
> Fresh-pulled corn cooked on the cob,
> Mashed potatoes with a great, big glob
> Of butter running as it melts,
> Buttermilk biscuits—better loosen your belts.
> Top it off with apple pie
> And ice cream piled on way up high:

That's what the Lord meant when he said
To ask Him for our daily bread.

Oh, yes—and don't forget a big, tall glass of iced tea, brewed with well water from Mom and Dad's old place, with a generous slice of lemon squeezed into it.

Well, maybe that is not *exactly* what the Lord was thinking of in first-century Palestine, but I'll bet Mary and Martha used to fix Him the ancient Jewish equivalent. We must bear in mind the fact that the Man who gave us this prayer is the same One who turned water into wine for a wedding party (John 2:1-11). He is the One who, when ev-eryone else was standing around open-mouthed at His raising of Jairus' daughter from the dead, asked that she be given something to eat (Luke 8:55). He was twice moved by compassion to multiply bread and fish for the multitudes, always making plenty to spare (Mark 6:30-44, 8:1-9); He treated His disciples to a fish fry (John 21:1-14); He instituted a symbolic meal as one of His followers' most central acts of worship (Matthew 26:26-30). Jesus was recognized by His disciples in the characteristic act of breaking bread (Luke 24:30-31) and undoubtedly blessed each of these meals in the words of that wonderful Jewish blessing, "Blessed art Thou, oh Lord, King of the universe, who dost cause bread to spring forth from the earth."

To include our daily bread in our prayers is to be reminded that the God we serve is, among other things, the God of sun and rain, seedtime and harvest, corn and wine. The ancients worshiped him mistakenly and corruptly as Ceres and Bacchus. But the true identity of the One who multiplies the fish in the sea, the corn in the ground and the grape on the vine was revealed in the miracles of Jesus. It is He who sends His rain on the just and the unjust and who makes glad the heart of men (Matthew 5:45, Acts 14:17, Psalm 104:10-30). Even after being cursed with thorns and thistles and the potential for drought and famine as a result of our sin, the earth in its fertility still speaks of His creative power and His goodness. Where we do not abuse it, it—or *He* through it—generally nourishes us with variety and abundance. And every time we stick something in our mouths, we should be reminded of what we owe Him.

If bread is a synecdoche for food, we can by the same figure legitimately expand the word to cover sustenance in general. All our material needs, everything which is physically required to sustain life and enable it to thrive is by implication included. The Lord specifically adds clothing in the immediate context (Matthew 6:25ff.), and it takes little imagination to include shelter as well. Consider the Father's goodness, Jesus says: The grass does not spin, but the lily is dressed better than Solomon, and won't your heavenly Father clothe you? Have a little faith, and stop worrying! The Father's *generosity* in these things is particularly stressed as an encouragement to bring these needs to Him in prayer.

The notion is not that we need not work, and

still less that we can expect God to load us up with lavish material wealth to spend on our lusts. It is rather that He does care about these practical necessities of life, that He made them for our enjoyment and that we can trust Him to take care of our needs. They are specifically the things which will be given to us when we put His kingdom first, as the prayer which immediately precedes this discussion will lead us to do. Therefore, not only may we ask, but it is precisely at the point in the prayer where this petition occurs that it is logical to do so, according to Matthew 6:33.

Bread for This Day

The bread we ask for is our *daily* bread. The word translated "daily" is a difficult one, the Greek *epiousios,* which occurs only in this passage. It probably means "the coming," i.e., bread for the day which is coming. It would have been appropriate for Jewish morning or evening prayer: either bread for the day which is now dawning or bread for the one which is coming tomorrow. Is this a prayer which is relevant for modern people who already have enough food in their cupboards, refrigerators and freezers to last for a week or more? Jesus was encouraging His disciples to trust God for their material needs one day at a time. And the position His disciples were in was literally one in which they had to do so. Today—this day, as every day—either God provides or I will not eat. There were times, as a struggling seminary or graduate student, that I lived that way literally. Usually we had at least peanut butter for a couple of days, but there were a few days we woke up literally not knowing where the next meal was coming from. Praying for my "daily" bread was a very meaningful act then, but is it equally so now that my refrigerator is fairly well stocked?

If we are people of understanding, it should be. Prosperity creates a feeling of self-sufficiency which is in reality nothing more than an illusion. The rich man in the parable thought he had goods laid up for many years to come, but his soul was required of him that very night and he never got to enjoy them (Luke 12:19-20). But even if he had lived to a ripe old age, his bigger barns were subject to moth, rust and corruption, not to mention fire and theft. The company with which it was all insured could go bankrupt, the bank could fail, indeed the whole economy within the context of which his wealth had meaning could crash into utter ruin overnight. It has happened to our own nation in the memory of many people still living, and in spite of the FDIC and other "safety nets" it could happen again. Even a simple power outage or mechanical failure while you're away from home for a few days can make the idea of corruption quite graphic when you reopen that well-stocked refrigerator.

The point is that whether wealth is consumed, stored or invested, we possess and enjoy it only by the grace of God. In the normal course of events there are certain precautions which are prudent, required of good stewards and usually rewarded with success—but there are no guarantees. All that is temporal is changeable, and in a fallen world the inevitable tendency of change is decay. Therefore, *this* meal that I eat *today* comes to me only by the good grace of my Lord. I am utterly dependent on Him for my ability to earn a living (Deuteronomy 8:18) and for the conditions of stability which allow me to enjoy the fruits of my labor. Only the normality and routine of this process make it hard to remember that this dependency is just as real and immediate as that of the pauper who lives hand-to-mouth. Whether my lunch is visible afar off in the pipeline or whether it comes to me out of the blue on the wings of ravens makes no essential difference. The fact that on this particular day I am able to enjoy it is something I owe entirely to my Father in heaven.

The Blessings of Bread: A Life of Thanks

This seemingly mundane petition is one which yields many blessings, of which our daily bread is only the beginning. The disciple who prays this petition with understanding receives an array of spiritual benefits as well. One of them is *a life of thanksgiving*. To pray daily for our physical and material needs is to be reminded daily of where they come from: "Every good and perfect gift is from above, coming down from the Father of the heavenly lights" (James 1:17). Though most of us must earn our bread by the sweat of our brow, still the ability to enjoy it is a gift from

God. To *ask* for it daily is to keep fresh in our
hearts the truth of our dependence and the recognition that each meal we receive is a token of
God's goodness and His love. It is to transform a
countless multitude of acts into occasions of worship, thanksgiving and praise: flipping on a light
switch, donning a sweater against the cold, pulling the covers up and stretching luxuriously in
bed at the end of day. Asking helps us understand that these physical comforts are not possessions to which our labor has given us a right;
they are gifts of the Father's grace, like Christ-
mas presents to be opened anew each day with
rejoicing and thanks.

The opportunity for thanksgiving is indeed not
the least part of the enjoyment of these gifts. One
of the greatest fringe benefits of being a Christian
is the fact that it gives us someone to thank. Without the feeling of gratitude which our delight in
good gifts should engender and leave behind, our
enjoyment of the gifts themselves is diminished.
But who does the non-Christian have to thank?
Only an impersonal force such as evolution or
chance. But what's the point in thanking an impersonal universe which really does not care
whether you enjoy its bounty or get crushed by
one of its natural upheavals? The secular person's
worldview contains no logical recipient of the
thanks which should logically be offered, and
hence for him the cycle of enjoyment is necessarily short-circuited. But the believer knows his
heavenly Father to be the only eligible recipient of

thanks for the gifts of creation and for our capacity to be blessed by them.

Thus for believers, as good gifts descend from the Father and thanks is returned upward, the cycle of enjoyment is complete. Every simple pleasure becomes an opportunity to reinforce the attitude of gratitude which transforms their whole outlook on life and positively enhances their childlike delight in all that God has made. And praying daily for their daily bread reminds them that this is their position in truth. Thanksgiving thus becomes the sauce which transforms just another meal into a feast and celebration of joy.

The Blessings of Bread: A Life of Faith

The second benefit of praying for our daily bread is *a life of faith*. To ask every day for our daily sustenance as if we started each day afresh with no resources of our own unmasks the illusion of prosperity and temporal security and teaches us the reality of living by trust in *God's* provision, not our own. It is not that planning ahead and providing for the future are wrong; in fact, they are required of us as good stewards of the blessings God has entrusted to us. It is not that we are not to do these things but that we are not to trust in them. My ultimate safety net is not my retirement program, disability insurance or IRA, certainly not Social Security or government welfare; it is my heavenly Father who can supply me with daily bread even if all these expedients fail. Indeed, if they succeed, it is He who is supplying that daily bread through them. And nothing is greater than the sense of liberation which such a practical life of faith provides.

The secular man works for his daily bread. He is therefore a slave to his job; without it he does not eat. Consequently, he tends to view his job as a means to an end. The end may include prestige, power and a false feeling of economic security. However he conceives it, his whole life and its value become defined in terms of possessing these things. How much of them is enough? Always a little bit more. So he works harder and longer to support his lifestyle, with the result that he has no time to use the toys his job has provided. He finds himself trapped in a vicious circle: He works in order to eat; he eats in order to live; he lives in order to work. But the last thing he can afford to do is to admit to himself that the whole process is a dead-end street. The one who dies with the most toys wins—but wins what? Nobody knows.

The disciple of Jesus who has learned to live by faith in terms of the Disciples' Prayer is set free from this rat race. He too works, but *not* for his daily bread. *He* works *for the glory of God*, not out of obligation but out of gratitude for God's grace. And he receives his daily bread, not from his job, but as a gift from his Father in heaven. Normally God will use his job as the channel through which to send his daily bread to him, but that is not the point of his working. The connection between his job and his bread is accidental, not essential. He would work even if he had no bills to pay, simply because he is a steward of his time and his gifts, which demand to be returned to the One who gave them. He works because there is good and useful and necessary work to be done for the good of his fellowman and the glory of his Maker, not for the petty goals of meaningless survival or the piling up of toys. Consequently his work has meaning as a part of his full life as a creature of the Creator, a servant of the Lord and a son of the Father. But he is not a slave to his job because he does not depend on it for his survival; if his employer fails, there is still his Father in heaven, who gives bread for the day simply out of the riches of the glory of his grace to those who are seeking first his kingdom.

Praying for our daily bread then gives us a life of faith, trusting God for our needs. This process liberates us not from responsibility or stewardship but from the chaos which awaits those who trust in their own devices. Faith is a confidence in the truth of God's words which leads to obedience. Jesus' original audience was probably reminded by the phrase *daily* bread of the manna God provided in the wilderness; it was literally "daily" bread, given for one day at a time. If you tried to hoard it, it rotted: "it was full of maggots and began to smell" (Exodus 16:20). But this would not happen on the day before the Sabbath; then you could gather twice what you needed and it would keep. But if you did not follow those instructions and make the required preparations for the Sabbath, you would find no manna on the ground and go hungry.

Israel's experience with the manna makes a perfect illustration of the freedom which comes from the obedience of faith when we trust our heavenly Father for our daily bread. For us as for the Israelites, it is not the bondage of legalism but the freedom of trust which allows us to resist the demands which our careers tend to make on time which should be reserved for our families or for worship and the service of God. It is the same trust in the goodness of our Father which sets us free from the temptation to push the boundary where good stewardship of our resources becomes greed or acquisitiveness for its own sake. What people did with the manna made visible their faith or lack of it. Those who had enough faith to believe what God said found manna a blessing, but for those who did not, it was only a frustration: rotten manna one day, none at all the next. And still as of old, that which we hoard contrary to the Lord's instructions has a tendency to go bad on us. It may not be today, and it may not be tomorrow, but sooner or later we will find it has bred worms: the worms of bitterness, jealousy, discontent, anxiety and fear which always breed in the carcass of greed. Why risk such a fate when God is so good? Work at your calling for the glory of God and trust Him for your daily bread, and enjoy the freedom of the life of faith.

The Blessings of Bread: A Life of Peace

The third benefit of praying this petition with understanding flows from the first two: it is *a life of peace*. "Therefore I tell you, do not worry about your life, what you will eat or drink; or about your body, what you will wear" (Matthew 6:25). The Gentiles eagerly seek for these things, and never rest secure in their possession of them; but the birds of the air and the lilies of the field are richly endowed with them by your Father in heaven, who cares even more for you—so don't be anxious! (See 6:32, 26-30.) Paul picks up the theme in Philippians 4:6-7: "Do not be anxious about anything, but in everything, by prayer and petition, with thanksgiving, present your requests to God. And the peace of God, which transcends all understanding, will guard your hearts and your minds in Christ Jesus." And the prayer one would logically pray is the one the Lord taught us. Prayed in faith, it relieves us of these anxieties and substitutes peace for them: "Give us this day our daily bread."

Summary

My children are not worried about where their next meal is coming from. They do not waste a single minute of their day fretting about whether I will have the money to pay the rent—or the light bill or the phone bill either. If they were a little older and knew a bit more about the condition of our checking account, perhaps they would! But for now their ignorance of the "real world" keeps them in a state of innocence and peace about these things. They have an unshakable trust and confidence that I will provide for their needs, and hence they live a life totally free from the worry I sometimes feel at the end of the month. The good news is that the peace they have out of ignorance is one we can enjoy out of knowledge: the knowledge of the character of our heavenly Father. His Son has told us that we can feel free to approach Him about any and every need we have. He has not promised to make our lives easy, but He has promised to supply all our needs, day by day, in Christ Jesus (Philippians 4:19). And that—if we really believe it—is the source of a peace of mind which passes understanding indeed.

Chapter 6

"Forgive Us Our Debts"

To prayer, repentance, and obedience due
Though but endeavored with sincere intent,
Mine ear will not be slow, mine eye not shut.

— John Milton, *Paradise Lost*

"Let the accused rise!"

The Judge's rich baritone reverberated through the halls of heaven, the corridors of hell and all the vast emptiness of space between. It commanded the attention of every sentient being, from the most exalted seraph to the lowest denizen of the deepest dungeon of Sheol, as the eternal doom of another son of Adam hung in the balance.

"You stand accused of high treason, of willful rebellion against your rightful Sovereign. You have done what you ought not to have done; you have left undone what you ought to have done;

101

and even in your good works you are guilty of idolatry, attempting to usurp for yourself the glory that belongs of right to your Creator. All your deeds, every thought, intent and secret motive of your heart, are a matter of public record in this court. How do you plead?"

"Guilty as charged, Your Honor. But I appeal from my guilt to Your grace through the cross of Jesus Christ."

"Your Honor, if I might approach the bench?" The Advocate's robes shone brighter than the sun, their brilliance serving only to highlight the scars in the palms of His hands. The two figures of splendor conferred briefly, and then the Judge's gavel rang like thunder.

"You are manifestly guilty, and the penalty is death. But I find that your account is paid in full. I therefore pronounce that you are pardoned and declare that this court considers you innocent of all charges. Enter into the joy of your Lord."

* * *

The Need of Forgiveness

Though our Savior teaches us to give first priority in our prayers to that which is of first importance—the glorious name, coming kingdom and sovereign will of God—He also teaches us to come to our heavenly Father with our personal needs. And central to those needs as developed by the Disciples' Prayer is what I do not hesitate to call the deepest, most urgent and most fundamental need of every person (but One) who has ever lived: the forgiveness of sins.

It is well that the Lord reminded us of our need for forgiveness. Had He not done so, our generation would surely have forgotten it. One of the greatest weaknesses of the Church in our day is the fact that the forgiveness of sin is no longer the focal point of Christian faith and experience even for an increasing number of conservative, Bible-believing people. No one can do pastoral counseling or personal work today without being confronted with the fact that this is true. And it is no wonder, for much of the preaching we hear is the proclamation of a vague gospel of personal fulfillment rather than the good news of salvation from God's wrath against sin through the blood of His Son.

This theological flabbiness in the Church reflects the relativism of the general culture. Jay Kesler, former president of Youth for Christ, noted in a recent speech that the biggest problem in evangelizing today's youth is the fact that they no longer have even the faintest concept of sin. Right and wrong are no longer categories with any objective meaning for them. The myth that modern technology and the secularization of modern society make the old morality outmoded is pervasively accepted. But the myth, believed, is powerful enough to continue to prevent our society from dealing with either reality or morality, in spite of rising tides of evidence that the two are connected after all. And the myth makes it hard for people to believe in sin or to feel sufficiently guilty for sin to make its forgiveness the life-or-death issue it is.

To appreciate this petition, we must begin by reminding ourselves of what sin really is. John defines it: "sin is lawlessness" (1 John 3:4). And that simple definition can be expounded in four basic propositions, four inescapable facts which govern our relation to the moral order of the universe.

The Law of God

The first is the fact that *God has a law*. This truth flows logically from our belief in a personal God, for a God who is a Person is a God who has a particular, definite and unchangeable *character*. That character is the source of all the laws which operate in the universe, for a "law" is simply a careful statement of one of the principles which form the content of God's character. Thus, the laws of logic are a reflection of His rationality—an imperfect reflection as they are codified by human beings, but a real reflection nonetheless. The laws of nature are a reflection of the orderliness of His creative mind in another way, or in another application. Likewise, the moral law reflects the ethical principles by which He operates and by which all of His creatures ought to live.

Because the moral law deals with the behavior of volitional and responsible creatures, it can be broken. The law of nature describes the way God has designed impersonal and inanimate bodies and forces to operate; because they are impersonal, they never deviate from that law in the normal course of things. But where human beings rise above the natural world, where we are like God in being personal and created in His image, we are also like Him in following His law not only by nature but by choice. The laws to which those choices apply are called the moral law. And precisely because it is that part of God's law to which choice is relevant, those creatures who are given the power of choice are capable of deviating from it. Because His character is the standard of goodness, when we deviate from it we commit evil and corrupt our own characters: in other words, we sin.

We know that God has a law, and in particular a moral law, not just because it stands to reason given the kind of Being He is, but because He has told us. He has summarized it for us in Scripture. In fact, He has given us several summaries which are mutually complementary. They include the Ten Commandments (Exodus 20:1-17), the Two Commandments (Matthew 22:35-40), the Sermon on the Mount (Matthew 5-7) and ultimately the character of Jesus Christ. These statements, in the context of the whole Bible, are the absolute standard of goodness, rightness and justice against which all of us must be measured. They are the law of God.

The Authority of God

The second fact is that *God as Creator has a right to our obedience*. It is not just that He has a character but that He commands and expects conformity

to the principles which flow from it, and He has
every right to do so. The biblical statements of the
law are descriptions of what He is morally like,
but they are also *commandments*, orders which we
as His creatures have an absolute, nonnegotiable
obligation to obey.

This proposition is indeed the sticking point for
our generation. We do not like authority; we prefer our independence, even at the price of damna-
tion. Nobody has ever expressed the attitude
better than A.E. Housman:

> The laws of God, the laws of man,
> He may keep that will and can;
> Not I: let God and man decree
> Laws for themselves, and not for me;
> And if my ways are not as theirs,
> Let them mind their own affairs.

"Mind your own business!" our collective consciousness cries out. "Don't try to impose your
morality on someone else!" The only virtue left is
open-mindedness, the only vice intolerance.

The only problem with this type of thinking is
that God *is* minding His own business when He
imposes His law on the cosmos. It is, after all, His
property; He made it. Most people still recognize
an individual's right to determine the use of anything he himself has made. If I write a book, I
have the right to negotiate a contract with a pub-
lisher for its production and sale. If you make
those arrangements without my consent and

authorization, you can end up in jail. What I cre-
ate (unless I use your materials without your permission) is mine to sell, give away or keep as I
choose. The general truth of this principle is self-
evident.

Well, God made me. I owe my existence entirely to Him. He did not even get the materials
from someone else. And I only continue to exist
by His good pleasure and sustaining power. He is
ultimate goodness, power and authority, the
source of all these things encountered in lesser beings. He is by nature, position and right my Creator and my King; I am His creature and His
subject. It does no good to complain that I never
consented to this arrangement; it is a simple given
of existence, a fact I have to deal with—much like
the necessity of breathing, and just as natural. Because of who we are, He has an inalienable right
to my obedience, and I have an irrevocable obligation to obey Him completely, freely and gladly. If
I do so I will fulfill my nature, and if I do not I
will twist and frustrate it. But the very nature of
the free obedience I owe Him makes it possible
for me to withhold it. Ever since our father Adam
committed us to that choice in the Garden, we
have done so grievously: we have sinned.

The Goodness of God

The third fact we need to remember is that *the
Law is good, and disobedience is therefore truly wicked
and inexcusable*. It is not just the transgression of
some arbitrary rule; it is not some peccadillo to be

sniffed at by a fastidious conscience; it is an evil, ungrateful rebellion against our good and gracious King. It is treason. By participating in this rebellion we make ourselves cancer cells eating away at the moral fabric of the universe, for we have set ourselves against the Source of everything that is good and wholesome and decent and beautiful. Our involvement keeps us from perceiving it as such, but we are enmeshed in something which is malicious, malignant and ugly, repulsive in its essential nature. And it is especially so to God Himself, the purity of whose character finds sin literally intolerable.

Moreover, He, who is the One principally affronted and offended by every sin, has done absolutely nothing to deserve such treatment at our hands. Yet the race is so enamored of sin that it hates Him and even has the nerve to defend itself by picturing Him as some sort of cosmic killjoy. One does not have to be Hitler, Stalin or Saddam Hussein to be in desperate need of forgiveness, for the tiniest sin partakes of the same inherently wicked nature as their more dramatic crimes, differing from them only in degree.

The Justice of God

The fourth fact is truly sobering in the light of the first three: *God is not only good and loving but also just, and must therefore reward sin with its appropriate punishment.* Adam was warned in the Garden that death would be the penalty for disobedience (Genesis 2:17). When he fell, he incurred that penalty on behalf of the entire human race, which has proceeded to ratify his choice by all its subsequent history. And still the wages of sin is death (Romans 6:23). Capital punishment is what sin deserves—not just particularly heinous crimes but *sin* deserves it. An everlasting death, eternal separation from God, is the right and just and appropriate sentence which God as the Judge of all the earth must pass on all who have disobeyed His law. To do otherwise would be neither honest nor just nor right nor even good, which is to say that it would be impossible, indeed unthinkable. Sin must be punished or God would not be God.

Now if these things are true, our position is a difficult one indeed. For it is undeniable that each one of us is a transgressor of the law—and not just in isolated instances but in the whole tenor and direction of our lives. Which of us keeps perfectly even the first commandment to have no other gods before the true God? For which of us, in other words, has God been constantly the most important thing in our lives? If we are honest, we must admit that *we* are the most important thing in our lives; we really want to be gods unto ourselves. We are, in fact, guilty not just of occasional misdemeanors but of high treason, of being chronic and habitual plotters of insurrection.

This being the case, our record with respect to the other commandments is not much better. Some of the more upright of us have avoided for the most part the outward and overt *acts* of murder, theft, adultery or false witness. But if Jesus' commentary on the law in the Sermon on the Mount is correct, if lusting, hating, coveting or lying to ourselves are the moral equivalents in God's eyes of the outward acts of adultery, murder, theft or false witness (Matthew 5:22, 28, etc.), then we are surely guilty of all. Our history, our natures, our dispositions and our daily choices all proclaim us as transgressors of the law, as sinners before a pure and holy God.

The Problem of Forgiveness

We begin to see then why the forgiveness of sin is the greatest need of men and women. Jesus speaks of sin as a debt: "Forgive us our debts as we forgive our debtors." We owe God a debt because we have sinned, and the debt will have to be paid—but we cannot pay it and live. So having that debt forgiven is the greatest need conceivable. And the Father, being a God of love, is kindly disposed toward us and would like to forgive that debt. But our greatest need then becomes the greatest problem of theology: How can a just God forgive the guilty? His justice demands that the penalty be paid as much as His love desires to release us. And so the greatest need of human beings and the greatest problem of theology becomes the greatest theme of Scripture: the gospel of Jesus Christ.

But before we rush on to the solution, we need to be sure we understand the problem: How can a just God forgive? If it does not seem like a problem to us, we do not yet understand our sin or

God's justice. We will never understand the Bible until we realize that we really deserve hell, and since God is just, we must have it. God is merciful and would like to forgive; He is just and must punish. "Without the shedding of blood there is no forgiveness" (Hebrews 9:22). How is this dilemma to be resolved? We will never understand the Bible as long as we seek a cheap and easy solution which does not reckon with the desperation and helplessness of our situation. There is no help to be found in ourselves; there is no work we could do, however meritorious, no sacrifice we could make, however great, which could put the situation right (Romans 3:20). If there is any solution it will have to come from God and God alone—but even Omnipotence cannot atone for sin without paying a price.

The Provision of Forgiveness

We have a debt which must be paid but which we cannot pay. In one way, the solution is simple: Someone else will have to pay it for us if we are to be released from it. But who could that someone be? He must be a man, for sin is a human condition and the death which is owed is a human death. He must be able to stand before God as a representative of all humankind if he is to make payment on our behalf. He must be personally innocent of sin—otherwise his death only pays for his own guilt and is of no avail to anyone else. And the life he offers up must be of infinite value, for he gives it in exchange, not just for another, but for all.

Where can we find a redeemer who meets these qualifications? Who is able and willing to give his own life, the innocent for the guilty, as a ransom for many? (Matthew 20:28). There is only one life of infinite value, able to absorb the death due a race of sinners and yet live, and that is the life of God Himself. And that indeed was God's solution—the only solution possible. God the Son, the second Person of the Trinity, would become a man. He would take on our nature, like us in every way except sin (Hebrews 4:15), while still remaining God.

And so that no one could ever say that God had merely winked at sin, shoving it under the rug because of His affection for the guilty (Romans 3:25), Christ took our place before the bar of judgment and suffered on our behalf the full penalty, paid as our substitute and representative the full debt so that God could forgive us without injustice. He is therefore able to issue a complete pardon to all those who will confess their sin and rebellion and receive the Pardoner as their Lord: "Therefore, there is now no condemnation for those who are in Christ Jesus" (8:1).

The key to life or death for us is simply this: Are we willing to admit that we need the forgiveness of sin, that God has provided it in Christ and that there is nothing we can do to obtain it except to ask in faith and receive? Yet this is a problem for us. To ask for forgiveness, we must first admit that we need it, and this is a blow to our pride. Or even if we recognize we have a problem, we prefer to try to work out another solution of our own. But there is no other solution. We must pray "forgive us our debts," putting our trust in Christ's work alone. When we do, we are forgiven. The word Paul uses in Romans is "justified" (Romans 3:24, 26, etc.). It means declared just, declared innocent, acquitted, set free. As far as God is concerned our sin is removed and therefore, through Christ our representative, we are restored to fellowship with Him.

Justification is something which happens once and for all when we receive the pardon, but the request for forgiveness is an ongoing part of the prayer the Lord composed for His disciples. That is because Christians are not perfect (yet)—just forgiven. When we turn to Christ we are restored to fellowship with God and released from the guilt and penalty of sin forever. In turning to Christ we turn from our sin; that is called repentance. We can no longer continue in the same old lifestyle of self-centered rebellion, for we are no longer our own, being bought with a price (1 Corinthians 6:20).

But we are not perfect, nor does our forgiveness depend on our being or becoming so. We sometimes still stumble and fall into sin. These lapses do not forfeit our pardon, which is wholly dependent on Christ's work, not our own, but they do impair our relationship with the Father. They are also painful to us, for knowing how much we owe to His unmerited favor, the last thing we want to do is transgress His will again. So we have a daily need of cleansing and forgiveness as part of the Christian life: as "we confess our sins, he is faithful and just and will forgive us our sins and purify us from all unrighteousness" (1 John 1:9).

Because He knew that our new relationship with the Father needs to be kept fresh and unimpeded daily, the Lord included the prayer for forgiveness in the Disciples' Prayer as well as the Sinners' Prayer. It is a rare day that any of us can say that we have not fallen short of the glory of God in any way. But having appropriated afresh the forgiveness which flows from Calvary, we can stand before the Father as innocent and guilt-free as Jesus Christ Himself. Thus the inclusion of this petition teaches us the importance of daily self-examination, confession and repentance as essential to our spiritual health. We do this not because we are morbid or defeated but because the Savior has invited us to come to Him for the daily renewal of the clean conscience which is among His greatest gifts to us. Indeed, a life of continual repentance is not the admission of defeat but the path to victory. If nothing else, it reminds us of how much we owe Him. For "God demonstrates his own love for us in this: While we were still sinners, Christ died for us" (Romans 5:8).

The Practice of Forgiveness

It is somewhat curious that this petition has attached to it a promise of action on our part. While there is nothing we can do to earn forgiveness except to ask, the authorized form of asking contains a commitment to do something: we ask to be forgiven our debts "as we forgive our debtors." This little phrase was apparently something the Lord considered to be of extreme importance, for as soon as He had finished giving the prayer He stopped to expound it: "For if you forgive men when they sin against you, your heavenly Father will also forgive you. But if you do not forgive men their sins, your Father will not forgive your sins" (Matthew 6:14-15).

But how can justification be a free gift received by grace alone through faith alone *apart from works* (Romans 3:23-24, 28, 6:23, Ephesians 2:8-10) and forgiveness be conditioned on a requirement which sounds suspiciously *like work?* Jesus plainly said that if we do not forgive we cannot be forgiven. C.I. Scofield in his famous annotated Bible even went so far as to declare these verses "legal ground," as if the Disciples' Prayer were not for believers under grace!

A much better answer is to say that of course Jesus and Paul were both right. There is nothing we can do to earn forgiveness, which comes only by grace through faith; but forgiveness of its very nature carries with it requirements of its own. It is quite true that God will not forgive me unless I forgive others, not because I must forgive them in order to win His forgiveness, but because I cannot really be forgiven in the New Testament sense without being forgiving. It is simply impossible to see oneself as a forgiven sinner whose pardon was bought by the infinitely precious blood of Jesus and simultaneously feel too good to forgive someone else. The two attitudes are mutually exclusive; it is not possible for them to coexist in the same mind at the same time. The contradiction would be intolerable.

This does not mean that believers will never struggle with forgiving those who have hurt them deeply; it simply means that ultimately their own forgiveness will demand that they do so. They will show whether they have truly reckoned with their own sinfulness and accepted God's pardon on a basis of pure grace and not their own merit by how they finally resolve the issue. If they can persist in refusing to forgive, they will show plainly that they themselves know nothing of the grace—the unmerited favor—of God.

Therefore, when we pray this petition of the Disciples' Prayer, making it personal and particular, we should examine ourselves concerning not only those things we need to be forgiven for, but also concerning those who need forgiveness from us. We should be reminded how incompatible an unforgiving spirit is with the stance which accepts a totally undeserved pardon purchased at such a high price to the Redeemer. We should ask for grace to forgive our own enemies from the heart, but where we find forgiveness difficult, we also can simply remind ourselves of the vast discrepancy between our own deserts and the way the Lord has treated us. In thanking and praising Him thus for our own forgiveness, we also find the ability we need to forgive others. And doing so confirms the fact that we ourselves are in a state of grace.

Summary

By including this petition in our model prayer, Jesus teaches us that self-examination, confession and repentance should be a regular part of our praying. Forgiveness is our deepest need; receiving it ought to be one of our deepest desires; the assurance that we have it ought to be among our deepest joys. So this part of the prayer is a time of sorrow for our sins but also of gratitude for God's grace and for luxuriating in His love. Here we lay hold of the Savior especially as the Friend of Sinners, the Lamb of God slain from the foundations of the world for His own, the Good Shepherd who laid down His life for the sheep, the One whom we love because He first loved us. If being the recipients of such love does not fill our hearts with joy, nothing can. There is no joy more exhilarating than the knowledge that there is now no condemnation for those who are in Christ Jesus (Romans 8:1) and the knowledge that we are included on the basis of His promise that those who come to Him He will never drive away (John 6:37). To have such knowledge is to be able to sing with David:

> Blessed is he
>> whose transgressions are forgiven,
>> whose sins are covered.
> Blessed is the man
>> whose sin the LORD does not count
>>> against him. . . .

When I kept silent,
    my bones wasted away
    through my groaning all day long. . . .

Then I acknowledged my sin to you
    and did not cover up my iniquity.
I said, "I will confess
    my transgressions to the LORD"—
and you forgave
    the guilt of my sin. . . .

Many are the woes of the wicked,
    but the LORD's unfailing love
    surrounds the man who trusts in him.

Rejoice in the LORD and be glad, you
        righteous;
    sing, all you who are upright in heart!
       (Psalm 32:1-3, 5, 10-11)

Chapter 7

"Deliver Us from Evil"

*Apollyon, beware what you do; for I am in the
King's highway, the way of holiness; therefore
take heed to yourself.*

—John Bunyan, *Pilgrim's Progress*

The country road was long, straight, lonely
and empty. The cruise control was set on
fifty-five, and I was on my way home from a
speaking engagement, anxious to get back. The
road cut straight across the rolling hills of the
Georgia piedmont. From the top of one hill you
could see a long way, but from the dip in between
on up to the top of the next, you didn't dare
pass—not that there was anyone to pass anyway.

There was a sleepy little gas station and general
store at the bottom of this particular hill. A beat-
up brown sedan was pulling away from the
pumps. OK, he sees me—he's slowing down to let

me go on by before he pulls out. No! Wait! The idiot is coming anyway! *Surely* he saw me.

I hit the brakes and the horn simultaneously. The horn had no effect, but the brakes sent all the loose items from the back of the station wagon flying up into the front seat. I don't know if the tires or the horn made more noise, but I'm sure the tires made more smoke. By God's grace, I missed his back bumper by at least three-eighths of an inch. Having been in such a hurry to enter the lane, he then proceeded down it at a leisurely fifteen miles per hour for about a hundred yards until he turned off into a dirt driveway. There was nothing coming behind me; by pulling out in front of me he had probably saved an entire five seconds at the cost of my nerves and half the tread on my tires. And I'm almost certain he knew I was coming.

Now, I must confess that my old Adamic nature suggested some uncharitable sentiments to me concerning this particular gentleman, including some rather uncomplimentary speculations about his ancestry and a recommended itinerary for his journey into the next life. When I realized I wasn't going to hit him, I knew I was being presented with a choice. I could indulge the sentiments, enjoy them—even shout them at the receding back of his neck as he inched into that driveway—perhaps nurse them and dwell on them the rest of the way home. Or I could repudiate them as unworthy of a servant of Jesus Christ and pray for him (and for the safety of anyone else traveling the same road) instead.

Did it really matter which I did? He probably wouldn't have heard me anyway.

Well, yes, it did matter. Either decision would leave a tiny mark on my own soul and leave me that much more predisposed toward or against Christlikeness the next time I was faced with such a choice—perhaps on an occasion in which somebody *would* hear.

Which choice would I make? Which would you have made? And what would determine that choice?

The Christian life begins with the forgiveness of sins, but it does not end there. For the Christ who died in our place, as our representative before the bar of God's justice to purchase our pardon, also rose from the dead. He now lives as our representative, our head and the captain of our faith to lead us on to victory over sin. While that victory will not be final and complete in this life, it is to be substantial. Because this continuing spiritual warfare is a part of our Christian experience, guidance and strength to pursue it are also a continuing need. Hence the final petition of the Disciples' Prayer: "Lead us not into temptation, but deliver us from evil."

The Definition of Testing

As was the case with the second petition, we have here another prayer which seems to have a dual focus but is really a single request. Avoidance of temptation, in other words, is not a separate concern requested for its sake, but is requested as a means to the ultimate goal of this part of the prayer: deliverance from evil. We might paraphrase it, "Instead of leading us into temptation, deliver us from evil." The focus is on the last part; the primary point is not so much avoidance of temptation as victory over it. But to appreciate why this is so, we need to understand how the two parts of the petition relate to each other.

That relationship is complicated by the fact that, taken by itself, the first part of this petition is highly problematic. Lead us not into temptation? But James says, "Consider it pure joy, my brothers, whenever you face trials of many kinds [or "temptations," KJV], because you know that the testing of your faith develops perseverance" (1:2-3). The same Greek word, *peirasmos,* which is translated "temptation" in Matthew 6:13, is also used by James and translated "temptation" or "trial" (James 1:2). James says to rejoice in *peirasmoi* (plural) because they produce endurance and spiritual maturity, and Jesus says to ask to be led around them. Why would Jesus ask to be spared something which James says is good for us?

The plot thickens further when James urges, "When tempted, no one should say, 'God is tempting me.' For God cannot be tempted by evil, nor does he tempt anyone" (1:13). Now James seems to be saying that God does not bring temptation into our lives in the first place; it comes from somewhere else. So why would Jesus tell us to pray that God not do something which James says He doesn't do anyway?

Mark Twain was aware of the problem these passages seem to present when he wrote his famous short story "The Man Who Corrupted Hadleyburg." The town of Hadleyburg prides itself on its reputation for honesty and incorruptibility. Its citizens strive to maintain integrity by shielding their children from even the temptation to dishonesty, going so far as to adopt "Lead us not into temptation" as the town motto. But a passing stranger, offended by their smugness, devises a plot to unmask their self-righteous hypocrisy once and for all. In a tour de force of ironic humor, Twain shows how their untested "virtue" is no virtue at all: Each of the principle citizens easily succumbs to the temptation arranged by the stranger because, having never needed to resist temptation before, they find that they have no resistance when the chips are down.

James, of course, was right. A certain amount of temptation is indeed good for us and necessary to our growth in grace. No one has ever put it better than Milton. "I cannot praise," he said, "a fugitive and cloistered virtue, unexercised and unbreathed, that never sallies out and seeks her adversity, but slinks out of the race." True virtue can be revealed only by adversity and pressure. Thus, "He that can apprehend and consider vice with all her baits and seeming pleasures, and yet abstain, and yet distinguish, and yet prefer that which is truly better, he is the true wayfaring Christian" *(Aeropagitica)*. That is why God does permit various tests, trials and temptations to come into our lives and why we should face them, not grudgingly, but with joy over the growth they can produce.

But Jesus was right too. It would be blasphemous to think otherwise. Yet what, in the light of the rather self-evident truth of James' teaching, could He have meant by "Lead us not into temptation"? If we can come to an understanding full enough to encompass both Jesus' insights and James', we may have the key to turning temptation into deliverance from evil.

The Purpose of Testing

One clue may be the word "temptation" itself. *Peirazo* can mean either to tempt, to entice to evil, or to try, i.e., to test. *Peirasmos* can mean either the temptation or a trial. And the fact that the one word can be translated both ways suggests that the two concepts are related: What may be a simple test of endurance for one person may be an insidious enticement to evil for another. It depends on how we respond. So part of the answer may be that Jesus and James are playing off different connotations of the word. We *will* have trials, in other words, but we can pray that when they must come they will not be for *us* an enticement to sin.

God does not tempt—He does not lure people into evil—but He does test and try His servants. "See, I have refined you, though not as silver; I have tested you in the furnace of affliction" (Isaiah 48:10). Satan, on the other hand, is definitely a tempter. He has a vested interest in getting us as enmeshed in evil as he can. He will consequently throw as many enticements at us as he can get away with. And God does permit him to do so. The very same event which Satan intends as a temptation, God may permit as a trial. The one has the goal of making us fall; the Other has the goal of strengthening us spiritually by letting us work against resistance, like a weight lifter. Which it will be depends on our response. But we need help from above to maintain the right attitude and make the right response—and the prayer the Lord taught us is designed to solicit that aid. "Don't lead us into temptation—but when the trials in Your wisdom are necessary and permitted, help us in them to overcome the evil possibilities inherent in them."

What's at Stake in Testing

It is interesting that the word "evil" in the second phrase has a definite article. It is *ho poneros*—literally, *the* evil. It is an expression which can very well mean "the evil one," or Satan himself. Both God and the devil take a personal interest in our trials and temptations. These experiences are a part of the cosmic spiritual war which rages between them, and we become at such moments the battleground, key positions to be taken or lost as the battle progresses. There are consequences for ourselves: Every victory of Satan twists, corrupts and destroys our natures and our potential for joy and fulfillment, while every victory of Christ strengthens us and deepens our capacity for the glory we were created to share with Him. But there are consequences for the cosmos as well. Satan's triumphs dim and blot out the light of the gospel in our lives, while Christ's burnish us and polish us as clearer and brighter beacons of His truth, shining before men and angels. The ultimate victory was won once for all by Christ on the cross, but the war still continues until His return. In the meantime, the key to how well the campaign is going seems to be *our prayers.* The victory is not in ourselves but in Christ as we pray, "Deliver us from the evil one."

God permits us to be tried not only for our growth but for His glory. Our temptations are an opportunity for the whole cosmos to see grace in action, the wonder of God triumphing over Satan, not through the direct exercise of His omnipotence but through weak vessels such as ourselves.

It is precisely our weakness which makes us such grand test cases for whether Satan or the Father will receive glory. Without controversy, the greater the difficulty of the task, the greater the glory which one accrues to the one who accomplishes it. That is why Olympic judges consider "degree of difficulty" when they compute gymnastics scores. So when God confronted the adversary directly and cast him out of heaven, it was a glorious victory indeed. But that triumph was nothing compared to the one which happens when His strength is made perfect in our weakness (2 Corinthians 12:9). It is important for our own sake that we do not yield to temptation, for the maintenance of our own personal sanctity and unbroken fellowship with the Father and enjoyment of His blessings. But there are far greater issues at stake in temptation than that.

For God to allow us to be tempted—with His own honor and glory at stake—is a costly decision on His part. Sometimes His children stumble and fall, bringing His name into disrepute. But through His grace they can stand, and in the long run those who truly belong to Him, who have been regenerated and are being transformed by His Holy Spirit, ultimately do stand. Our Father then permits trials and temptations to come into our lives because He has high hopes for us. All the hosts of heaven wait with bated breath to see what we will do. For when we trust in the Lord rather than in our own strength and emerge like Job victoriously, our relationship with the Father is deepened, our own spiritual lives are strengthened and the devil is sent packing in disgrace. And God is glorified.

Passing the Test

What an encouragement this should be to us! It does not matter what the struggle may be. Whatever outward circumstances conspire with the weakness of our own natures and the solicitations of the enemy to discourage us, put pressure on us or otherwise allure us to unfaithfulness, the struggle is not with flesh and blood (Ephesians 6:12). Therefore the victory does not depend on flesh and blood or on our own weak and corrupt natures. Someone is pulling for us, cares for us, believes in us and stands ready to aid us. He has promised that He will not allow the trial to be more severe than what we—in Him—can bear (1 Corinthians 10:13). He is in our corner. He has already given the blood of His Son to make our victory possible. And that Son, resurrected from the dead and given all power and authority in heaven and on earth (Ephesians 1:19-22), now re-sides in us who believe through His personal agent and representative, the Holy Spirit. That is Christ is us, the hope of glory (Colossians 1:27). Therefore, He encourages us to pray, "Lead us not into temptation, but deliver us from the evil one."

The Disciples' Prayer then is the key to victory over Satan in temptation. That is, the key to spiri-tual victory is the confession of our weakness and dependence and the invocation of the Father's aid and protection. Conversely, presumption—the tendency to meet these challenges with the arm of flesh, thinking that we are in ourselves sufficient to handle them—is the key to defeat.

So one of the functions of the twofold way in which this petition is expressed is to guard us from presumption. We begin our petition for aid with the confession of our weakness: "Lead us not into temptation." We know there will be plenty of temptations in our experience, but what we are doing before God is eschewing a kind of spiritual machismo which says, "Hey, bring 'em on! I'm ready for them!" No. Acknowledging our weak-ness, we asked to be spared those which are not necessary even as we plead for deliverance in those which are.

As usual, we find the model prayer the Lord gave us to be supremely logical and beautifully adapted to our needs. We will not pray for deliverance as seriously as we ought until we have reckoned with our need for it, until our attitude toward temptation in general is a proper one. The Bible is full of healthy admonition on this score. "So, if you think you are standing firm, be careful that you don't fall!" (1 Corinthians 10:12). "Pride goes before destruction, a haughty spirit before a fall" (Proverbs 16:18). "Apart from me you can do nothing" (John 15:5). The truth is repeated because we continually need to hear it; we are suicidally prone to ignore it. But when we use the Disciples' Prayer as the Lord's outline for our praying, we will be reminding ourselves of this truth daily in the presence of the Father.

Testing and Growth

This prayer was given for God's children to use with their heavenly Father, and it was also given to Jesus' disciples by the Master. Since the disciple-master relationship is basically a learner-teacher relationship, it might be useful to look at some insights which the process of education can give us into the process of spiritual "testing." A good exam question is not designed to trip the student up (though it may have that effect if he is unprepared!), but to give him an opportunity to show what he has learned, to put it use. And the primary purpose of the test is not to pass or fail the student (spiritual tests are passed only by grace anyway), but to reveal to him how he is doing. He may think he has learned the material, but seeing how little of it he is actually able to get down on paper on the midterm may inspire him to hit the books a bit more seriously before the final exam.

Likewise, the Father tests His children, and the Lord His disciples, for their good, as a means to their further growth. God does not need to know how our spiritual growth is progressing, but we do, and the only way we can find out is to be tested. And what does the test reveal? What is the Father saying to us through the trials He permits? What is His reply to our prayer of "Lead us not into temptation, but deliver us from evil"?

When we do fall into temptation, perhaps we can hear Him saying something like this: "Well, you are not the spiritual hotshot you thought you were, are you?" There may be specific personal applications. "Been missing your devotions lately? Sunday-morning Christianity really isn't enough, is it? Depending on your own strength and wisdom lately? Or have you been *inviting* temptation through the things you watch, read or listen to or the places you go?" (Surely one benefit of daily asking God not to lead us into temptation is to realize how inconsistent it is with this request for us to lead *ourselves* into temptation! It will certainly come, but it is not our place to seek it out.) Or, if none of the above is applicable, it may be nothing more than this: "Hey—remember, you still need Me after all." And, definitely and always, Christ is saying, "Come back, and all is forgiven. I'm on your side; I want to help you. You cannot overcome the evil one, but I can. Together, therefore, *we* can. Come on, let's start over."

And when we do stand, we may undoubtedly hear the Father saying something like this: "Well done, thou good and faithful servant! See, I told you all along that we would overcome if you would totally trust in Me. I am so pleased with your progress! Now I want you to grow even stronger in Me and not to forget that apart from Me you can do nothing. So watch out; another test will be coming. But I will be with you there as I was here. In the meantime, you keep right on praying, 'Lead me not into temptation, but deliver me from evil.' "

Amen.

Chapter 8

"For Thine Is the Kingdom"

Of all the creatures both in sea and land
Only to Man thou hast made known thy ways,
And put the pen alone into his hand,
And made him secretary of thy praise.

— George Herbert, *The Temple*

The faith-promise pledge cards for world missions had been collected and tallied and the figure had been handed to the pastor. And it was obvious that God had done a tremendous work, for the figure was far greater than anyone had the faith to hope for. God's kingdom had just been advanced by His power, for His glory, and the victory could not just be announced but had to be celebrated. Hardly needing any direction, the whole congregation rose to their feet as the organist began the introduction:

* * *

Praise God from whom all blessings flow;
Praise Him, all creatures here below;
Praise Him above, ye heavenly host;
Praise Father, Son, and Holy Ghost!

If we really understood the power and nature of
the One to whom we pray, if we really understood the nature of prayer, its privilege and power,
then we would be compelled to end even our most
mundane, routine, daily prayers on just such a
note. For *doxology* means literally "a word of
glory." It is the essence of worship, the ascription
of all glory, honor, power and praise to our Father
in heaven because He alone is worthy.

The doxology at the end of the Disciples'
Prayer, "For thine is the kingdom, and the power,
and the glory, for ever. Amen" (Matthew 6:13,
KJV), is not in the earliest manuscripts of the
Gospel of Matthew. Neither is it mentioned in the
earliest patristic commentaries on the Lord's
prayer, by men such as Tertullian, Origen or
Cyprian. Most scholars believe that it was not a
part of the original prayer, but was added by the
early Church as it adapted the prayer for use in
public worship. The fact that several different versions of the ending exist in the manuscripts adds
weight to this conclusion. We may safely conclude
that the prayer as the Lord gave it ended with the
petition to be delivered from evil, much as Luke's
version does (Luke 11:1-4). What then should be
our attitude toward these final words as we use
the Lord's model prayer today?

I would suggest that we should accept these concluding phrases for what they are: not the Lord's words to us, but the words of His early disciples to Him. And they are good words, words which His disciples still do well to ascribe to Him today. The prayer, if we have understood it correctly, was a guide or a model which the Lord *intended* His disciples to expand and elaborate on according to their needs. This earliest such elaboration was so appropriate that it has by tradition become a part of the prayer itself. It is important for us to know what was part of the original and what was not, for the Lord's words and those of His apostles are our final court of appeal. But we can continue to use the early Church's praise as the appropriate conclusion to the prayer, as part of the text from which *we* elaborate, as long as we understand what we are doing and why.

In fact, the prayer as Jesus gave it needs, almost demands, some such conclusion. The prayer really never concludes—it just stops. It is almost as if the Lord deliberately left it open-ended, as if there were something in it He wanted us to supply ourselves, some response He wanted our communion with the Father to elicit from us naturally and spontaneously. The early Church was not slow to respond, and their response was worship. In this they set us an example which has never been bettered. The traditional ending summarizes the thrust of the whole prayer and brings it full circle in three great ascriptions of worth to the Father. His—and His alone—is the kingdom, the power and the glory—forever.

Thine

"*Thine* is the kingdom . . . power . . . glory." They are, first of all, *His*—uniquely His—His by nature. It is because they belong to Him that we can pray to Him; it is out of His inexhaustible possession of them that He answers our prayers; it is for His inalienable monopoly in them that we offer Him our praise and worship. Their existence in Him is the basis of prayer; their application to us is the enablement of prayer; and their manifestation in the world is the goal of prayer. Jesus came and shed His blood that we might enter His kingdom, experience His power and share His glory (Matthew 5:20, Ephesians 1:19, John 17:22). Jesus' prayer began with a concentration on who God is—our Father in heaven whose name is to be hallowed. And the ending supplied by the early Church returns the prayer full circle to that most basic focus. Who is God? He is the One whose nature overflows with kingdom, power and glory.

Kingdom

"Thine is the *kingdom*." As we saw, *kingdom* basically means *reign* or *rule (basileia)*. *Basileia* involves the combined ideas of the inherent right to rule and the actual exercise of that right. At the end of the prayer we confess that all rule, authority and sovereignty belong to God. All legitimate human authority, whether in the home, school or state, flows from Him. It is accountable to Him and owes its legitimacy to His delegation. It is under Him and loses its right to our obedience when it transgresses His law. He is the ultimate source of order, harmony, responsibility, freedom and human rights. None of these things would exist in human society apart from Him, and where we do enjoy them it is He who is to be praised. He is our king; He has already put all things beneath the foot of His Son (Ephesians 1:22). The day is coming when that reality will be manifested in all its completeness. The kingdom has come and is coming because Jesus Christ is Lord and our God reigns. Rule is His, and the wonder of wonders is that this King of kings is the One we began by addressing as our heavenly Father.

Power

"Thine is the kingdom, and the *power*." This is not *exousia*, the word often translated "power" but which really means "authority"—the idea of authority is already included in the earlier word for "kingdom," *basileia*. The word here is *dunamis*, from which descends the English *dynamo* and *dynamite*. Its meaning in Greek is the ability to get things done. In other words, God not only has the right to rule but the power to back up His exercise of that sovereignty. The theologians call it *omnipotence*: ultimate power. It was He who created everything else which exists. There is no power in the universe which does not derive its power from Him. There is therefore no power which is able to thwart His decrees. Is this God able to answer our prayers? He "is able to do immeasurably more than all we ask or imagine" (Ephesians 3:20). His is the power.

Glory

"Thine is the kingdom, and the power, and the *glory*." *Doxa* means majesty, grandeur, fame or good report. When applied to God it refers to the manifestation in the cosmos of His character in all its wisdom, goodness, justice, holiness and splendor. It is the cloud of brightness surrounding Him which no mortal eye can pierce. It is the burning purity of His nature as it impresses humans with the weight of His awesomeness. To be glorious is to be majestically and resplendently and eminently worthy of all honor, dignity, worship and praise. It may be the most basic and essential attribute God has—or maybe it is better to call it the sum of all the others.

Moses aspired to see it, but could only glimpse the tail end of it lest the full vision be more than he could bear, for no one can see God's face and live (Exodus 33:18-23). Even the angels are abashed before it. It dazzled the physical eyes in the smoke and lightning of Sinai, but it was revealed most clearly to the spirit in the life, death and resurrection of Jesus, who is its living embodiment (John 1:14). It is the glory of God that we fall short of when we sin, and to which we will be restored when our redemption is complete. Jesus' most astounding promise was that He would share it with His chosen ones, and that promise will be fulfilled when they hear the Father who is the source and possessor of all glory say to them, "Well done, good and faithful servant!" (Matthew 25:21, 23). They will respond by returning that glory to the One to whom it belongs, casting their crowns at His feet (Revelation 4:10). The early Church could not have done a better job of rounding off the prayer, because to ascribe glory to the Father is the essence of worship, and when we do it as the climax of the Disciples' Prayer we anticipate the worship of heaven on that Day perhaps more profoundly than at any other time except our celebration of the Lord's Supper.

Forever

"For thine is the kingdom, and the power, and the glory, *forever*." God possesses these attributes eternally. He has had them forever. He never got them from anyone else, and hence He can never lose them; they will be His forever. The God who opened the Red Sea for Israel and who opened the tomb for Jesus is still the same God of sovereignty, power and glory today that He was then—and He will be the same God tomorrow as well. Therefore the relationship with the Father, of which our prayers are the heartbeat, is eternal too. Thus we ironically end the prayer on a note which recognizes that the prayer does not in fact end; it is ongoing, indeed eternal, because the relationship it expresses is eternal. It continues ringing in the ears of the Father until we are able to return to it consciously. Kingdom, power and glory are God's—and hence the benefits which flow from them are His people's—forever. It is little wonder that some Greek manuscripts got so excited they said forever and *ever*.

Amen

"*Amen*." Amen means "so be it." It means much more than "OK, the prayer is over now, so you can open your eyes." It means that, having acknowledged God's possession of and inherent right to the kingdom, the power and the glory, we also confess it and affirm it. We say from the depth of our souls that we are glad to have it so, that we *want* all the sovereignty, power and glory to be His and not ours. We are no longer resisting His rule, trying to live by our own power and striving to take credit for whatever good there is in us. We stamp as the final period at the end of the prayer a resounding and joyful "Yes!" to God: to everything He is, to whatever His answer to our petitions may be, to whatever form His will for our lives may take. We do this because our communion with the Father along the lines that the Son laid down for us has convinced us that the kingdom, the power and the glory *are* His forever.

Amen.

Amen.

Amen.

"The Disciples' Prayer"

Oh Thou whose thoughts are far above my own
As are the stars above this whirling stone
We call the earth; who know'st the thoughts I
*   think*
Before I think to think them, though I shrink
To let Thee see them all; whose soul doth burn
With purity, and more, whose heart doth yearn
To see that flame of love also in me—
When I bow down before Thee on my knee,
What words have I that would be fit to say?
He said, "Just Father, Abba Father, pray."

So: that which I could never have begun,
Thou, sending forth Thine own beloved Son,
Hast done, accomplished: washed my sins away
So that as Thine adopted child, I may
Approach Thy throne—yet where shall I begin?
My purest thoughts are tainted yet with sin.

And though Thy Spirit stirs my heart to pray,
To such a One as Thou, what shall I say?
Show me my deepest need, my highest aim!
He said, "Begin with 'Hallowed be Thy name.' "

Yes! Reverently to set Thy name apart,
Grant it the highest place in all my heart,
And crown it there because it speaks of Thee,
Thy greatness and Thy grace poured out on me;
And so to come into Thy courts with praise
And in Thy gates my thanksgiving to raise—
Ah, nothing less than this my heart could give:
To crown Thee King of all my life—and live.
And what is next, now that I have begun?
"Just this: 'Thy kingdom come, Thy will be
                done.' "

Oh Thou who rulest in the heavens above
Where angels, burning with reflected love,
Flit forth like wings of wind or flames of fire,
Thy will their only thought, their sole desire;
If only I could be Thine instrument
On earth as they in heaven, with pure intent!
Since I believe Thy promise to be true,
Do Thou work in me both to will and do
Thy pleasure. What more can I ask? He said,
"Fear not to ask Me for your daily bread."

Thou who didst go to Calvary and bleed
To purchase everything that I might need—
What wondrous condescension this, that Thou

Should'st stoop ev'n to concern Thyself with how
I am to be kept, housed, and clothed, and fed!
How sumptuously Thine earth produces bread
For sparrows! And Thou causest it to yield
A wardrobe for the lilies of the field.
And yet, how soon Thy goodness we forget!
As we our debtors, please forgive our debt.

He said, "I do forgive you every whit
Your sin, for Jesus paid the price for it,
And you have freely bowed to Him as Lord
As evidenced by this, your very word
In asking for forgiveness; further still,
Your wish to pray according to My will
And for My glory." What else should I request?
For Thou alone does know just what is best.
He said, "Into temptation lead us not,
But save us from the devil's evil plot."

Thus do I pray, and thus shall ever pray:
From Thy dear side, Lord, let me never stray.
For I am weak and prone to every sin
Unless Thou cleanse me constantly within.
Oh, sanctify me with Thy Truth, lest lies
Of Satan tempt. Teach me to keep my eyes
Fixed ever on Thy Word, and thus on Thee.
For Thou alone, and nought that is in me,
Alone Thy greatness and Thy sovereign grace
Can save and keep me 'til I see Thy face.

For Thine it is to rule o'er everything,
Thine alone the kingdom, Thou the King;
Thou art a shield, a rock, a fort, a tower,
Thou burning strength, Thine all alone the
          power;
And every line of the salvation's story
Shouts Mercy! Grace! and Glory! Glory! Glory!
What Thou hast been, forever Thou wilt be,
And I Thy grateful slave on bended knee.
So be it: I, who once loved self and sin,
Delight to have it so; and so, amen.

                                        —D.T.W.

A Bibliographical Essay

Learning without piety will only make you more capable of promoting the kingdom of Satan. Henceforward, therefore, I hope you will enter into your studies not to get a parish, nor to be polite preachers, but to be great saints. This indeed is the most compendious way to true learning.

— George Whitefield,
Exhortation to American Students

This study can claim to be nothing more than appetizer. The main course must be a lifetime of growth in the use of the Disciples' Prayer as the Lord designed. But there is a host of other side dishes which can enhance the meal if they are used wisely. The menu which follows, though extensive, does not pretend to be exhaustive. It avoids works which, though useful, are highly technical and concentrates on those which, though challenging, might be helpful to the intelligent layperson. Many worthy treatments are absent due to my own ignorance, but those which are included are ones which I have found personally to be of value.

Commentaries

Most obviously useful, of course, are commentaries on the texts of the prayer itself or the Sermon on the Mount, which contains it. There can be no better place to start than John Calvin's *Harmony of the Evangelists, Matthew, Mark, and Luke*, vol. 16 of the twenty-two-volume set of *Calvin's Commentaries* reprinted by Baker in 1981. Calvin, the great Reformer, was also a great pioneer of the sound grammatico-historical method of exegesis. Not only was he a man of deep spiritual and theological insight, but his interpretive instincts were amazingly perceptive. He discusses both Matthew's and Luke's versions of the prayer together.

No one packs more spiritual nourishment into fewer words than J.C. Ryle in his *Expository Thoughts on the Gospels* (1856; rpt. Baker, 1977). A.B. Bruce, in chapter 6 of his classic *The Training of the Twelve* (1894; rpt. Kregel, 1977), examines the Disciples' Prayer in context of the Lord's general teaching about prayer. G. Campbell Morgan's discussion in *Great Chapters of the Bible* (Revell, 1935) is concise and right to the point.

In modern commentaries which combine sound exposition with spiritual application, D. Martyn Lloyd-Jones' *Studies in the Sermon on the Mount* (InterVarsity, 1959; rpt. Eerdmans, 1979) is unsurpassed. Chapters 2 and 4-6 deal with our topic. A recent commentary on Matthew which is weak on the doctrine of Scripture but strong in textual insight and evangelical warmth is F. Dale Bruner's *The Christbook: A Historical-Theological Commentary on Matthew 1-12* (Word, 1987).

Theology

Few systematic theologies give detailed attention to the theology of prayer. Of those who do, none is more profound than Calvin in chapter 20 of *The Institutes of the Christian Religion* (1559; trans. Henry Beveridge, 1845; rpt. Eerdmans, 1975, vol. 2, pp. 143-201). None is more detailed and thorough than Thomas Watson, the Puritan father whose treatment takes up fully one-third of his *A Body of Divinity* (1692; rpt. in modern times in its entirety by Sovereign Grace, n.d., and the section on the Lord's Prayer alone by Banner of Truth, n.d.). Modern discussions worth looking at include those of Hodge, *Systematic Theology* (1871-73; rpt. Eerdmans, 1975, vol. 3, pp. 692-709); Dabney, *Lectures in Systematic Theology* (1878; rpt. Zondervan, 1972, pp. 713-25); and Strong, *Systematic Theology* (1907; rpt. Revell, 1970, pp. 433-39). Jay Adams' *More Than Redemption: A Theology of Christian Counseling* (Baker, 1979) treats the theology of prayer in relation to counseling in chapter 6, but his treatment contains much of practical benefit which can be applied personally as well.

Prayer and Spirituality

Any study of prayer must ultimately relate it to the study of spirituality in general. Of many excellent books available on this topic, I will mention

only five. The indispensable classic here is
Jonathan Edwards' *A Treatise Concerning Religious
Affections* (1746; rpt. Yale, 1959). In this defense of
the first Great Awakening, Edwards provides a
profound and penetrating analysis of the criteria
by which we can discern true spirituality from its
counterfeits. More recent books which are worthwhile include Francis Schaeffer, *True Spirituality*
(Tyndale, 1971); J.I. Packer, *Keep in Step with the
Spirit* (Revell, 1984); and D. Martyn Lloyd-Jones,
Revival (Crossway, 1987). Finally, my *The Person
and Work of the Holy Spirit* (Broadman & Holman,
1994) provides a systematic overview of the work
of the Holy Spirit in the Christian life from a
thoroughly Christocentric perspective, relating it
to the need for personal and corporate reformation
and revival today. It stands with the present work
in attempting to provide the Church with a practical theology of the Christian life and Christian experience.

The Parts of Prayer

We then move to specific issues raised by the
parts of the prayer. The address asks us to consider whom we pray to. Aside from the discussions of the nature of God in the standard
systematic theologies, two other books deserve
mention. The great classic in this area is Puritan
Stephen Charnock's *The Existence and Attributes of
God* (1682; rpt. Baker, 1979). He not only explains
in rich detail the attributes themselves, but, like all
the great Puritans, delves deeply into the rele-

vance of these theological truths for practical Christian living. A modern book well on its way to becoming a classic is J.I. Packer's *Knowing God* (InterVarsity, 1973). His discussion particularly of the Fatherhood of God is especially nourishing. Since the divine name is the revelation of the divine Person, these materials will enrich our appreciation of the first petition as well.

"Thy kingdom come"—the best scholarly treatment of the doctrine of the kingdom is that of G.R. Beasley-Murray; the best popular treatment is George Eldon Ladd's *The Gospel of the Kingdom* (Eerdmans, 1961). A good short paperback is *God's Kingdom for Today*, by Peter Toon (Cornerstone, 1980). Much useful material on this topic will also be found in Ladd's *A Theology of the New Testament* (Eerdmans, 1974).

The theology and baking of our daily bread is discussed delightfully and daringly by Father Robert Farrar Capon in *The Supper of the Lamb* (Doubleday, 1969). Let fundamentalist teetotalers not be put off from enjoying the feast Capon serves up by the wine (and stronger things) he serves with it. They will miss a blessing if they do.

On the forgiveness of debts, the increasing evangelical flabbiness on the doctrine of sin (and other things too) is documented by James Davison Hunter in *Evangelicalism: The Coming Generation* (University of Chicago Press, 1987). The pervasive reality and seriousness of sin is recognized even by a secular psychiatrist in Karl Menninger's *Whatever Became of Sin?* (Hawthorn, 1973). Of many works on the atonement, three that are especially rich in insight are James Denney's classic *The Death of Christ* (1901; rpt. Tyndale, 1973), John Murray's *Redemption Accomplished and Applied* (Eerdmans, 1955; rpt. 1980), and John R.W. Stott's *The Cross of Christ* (Eerdmans, 1986).

On the practical aspects of living the Christian life and resisting the temptations of the enemy, I can recommend nothing better than Francis Schaeffer's *True Spirituality*, mentioned above. My *The Person and Work of the Holy Spirit* also attempts a practical theology of the Christian life. On the consequences of our increasing naivete and weakness in this area, Schaeffer's *The Great Evangelical Disaster* (Crossway, 1984) seems more prophetic today than it did when it was written.

Prayer and Praise

The conclusion of the prayer brings us back to the practice of praise; bibliographically it brings us to a theme stressed earlier in the study, the need to avail ourselves of the bountiful heritage of devotional literature which our forebears in the faith have left us. Prayers of praise, confession or intercession whose words we can make our own, lyrical discussions of the Father's greatness and His grace and other forms of practical help to our own praise and devotion abound in rich profusion in this vast body of literature of which the Church remains mostly ignorant. Of that body we can only search the surface in this essay; but here are some highlights.

Resources from the Past

Perhaps the most basic resource in this area is The Book of Common Prayer, or simply The Prayerbook, as it is sometimes known (published by the Protestant Episcopal Church in the U.S. in many editions). One does not have to be an Episcopalian to appreciate the sonorous and balanced phrases and the warm, evangelical theology of most of its prayers, meditations and services. Indeed, almost every Protestant denomination has paid it the ultimate compliment of borrowing its wedding ceremony, if nothing else, for its own use.

Going back to the patristic period, what may be the greatest devotional classic—certainly the greatest spiritual autobiography—of all time is St. Augustine's *Confessions*, published in any modern editions including one by Zondervan (1967). The whole book is really a prayer addressed to God in praise for His work in Augustine's life.

The best of medieval piety is seen in Thomas à Kempis' *The Imitation of Christ* (many modern editions). An excellent anthology of late medieval spiritual writing has been translated and edited by David Lyle Jeffrey in *The Law of Love: English Spirituality in the Age of Wycliffe* (Eerdmans, 1988).

The sixteenth century, the age of the Reformation, was necessarily a time in which doctrinal and polemical literature flourished more so than devotional writing. But many people find a theological classic like Calvin's *Institutes* more stimulating to devotion than most expressly "devotional" books. And the age did produce Cranmer's Prayerbook, the unsurpassed liturgical classic which has already been mentioned. A collection of *Christian Prayers and Holy Meditations* from that era in England was made by Henry Bull in 1566 and reprinted by the Parker Society in 1842. It is frequently available in major libraries which have the Parker Society reprints on the shelf.

The great age of Protestant devotional literature was beyond a doubt the seventeenth century. Two fascinating books on literary history explain why this was so. Louis Martz in *The Poetry of Meditation* (Yale, 1962) relates the remarkable flowering of devotional poetry to the literary application of techniques of meditative devotion inherited from the middle ages. Barbara Keifer Lewalski's magisterial *Protestant Poetics* and the *Seventeenth-Century Religious Lyric* (Princeton, 1979) complete the picture by showing how the literature was the natural outflow of Reformation doctrine and the Protestant approach to Scripture. In addition, I try to make some application of their insights to the problems of devotional writing in the late twentieth century in "Thou Art Still My God": George Herbert and the "Poetics of Edification," *Christian Scholar's Review*, 19:3 (March 1990), 271-85; rpt. in *Inklings of Reality* (Toccoa, GA: Toccoa Falls College Press, 1996), pp. 171-200.

Who were these writers? They include both the great literary Anglicans like Donne, Herbert, Vaughan, Traherne, Andrewes or Taylor, and the great Puritans like Bunyan, Baxter, Sibbes, Brooks and Boston. Increasingly at odds over ecclesiology, they shared a common perspective on the fundamentals of the faith. Known mainly to two different sets of people today, each has a great deal to offer all of us. The Anglicans are the ones who tend to show up in literature anthologies and college literature courses, often taught by secular professors with little understanding of or sympathy for their spiritual content. They also receive more attention from writers like Martz or Lewalski—rightly so, since their work is of generally greater merit from a purely literary standpoint. The Puritans, less elegant but deeply practical in their approach to spiritual life, have received increasing attention from reformed evangelicals in recent years. Two excellent introductions to their work and ministry are available in Leland Ryken's *Worldly Saints: The Puritans As They Really Were* (Zondervan, 1986) and J.I. Packer's *A Quest for Godliness: The Puritan Vision of the Christian Life* (Crossway, 1990). The best history of the movement in my mind is William Haller's *The Rise of Puritanism* (Columbia, 1938). Also of interest is D. Martyn Lloyd-Jones' *The Puritans: Their Origins and Successors* (Banner of Truth, 1987). Many of the works of the principal figures have been reprinted by Banner of Truth Trust.

An excellent sampling of the period can be found in Witherspoon and Warnke, *Seventeenth-Century Prose and Poetry*, 2nd ed. (Harcourt Brace, 1982). A few of the many authors represented there whose works are worth pursuing in more detail include Lancelot Andrewes, the famous preacher and member of the translation committee which worked on the King James Bible. His prayers have been collected by Alexander Whyte in *Lancelot Andrewes and His Private Devotions* (Baker, 1981). John Donne's prose and poetry are available in many editions, but Herbert H. Umbach collected his prayers in *The Prayers of John Donne* (Bookman, 1951). Jeremy Taylor's *The Rule and Exercises of Holy Living* is available in a modern edition from Harper and Row (1970). Perhaps least known by the average evangelical but arguably most valuable is George Herbert, whose complete works are edited by F.E. Hutchinson (Oxford, 1941). Finally, an inexpensive collection of the best of Puritan Richard Baxter is available in *The Practical Works of Richard Baxter: Select Treatises* (Baker, 1981).

The eighteenth century began as an age of great spiritual darkness. The classical orthodoxy of the seventeenth century was thought to have been discredited by the religious violence of the English Civil War, and Rationalism had arisen to fill the vacuum. But out of that darkness came the renewal of evangelical piety and faith known as the first Great Awakening, which produced a flowering of devotional and spiritual writing second only to that of the seventeenth century. David Lyle Jeffrey has given us an outstanding anthology of those writings in *A Burning and a Shining Light: English Spirituality in the Age of Wesley* (Eerdmans,

1987; rpt. as *English Spirituality in the Age of Wesley*, Eerdmans, 1996). Any hymnbook also constitutes an anthology of the best of this era, as the words of Watts, Newton, Cowper and Charles Wesley deservedly continue to be staples of our worship. Complete works from the period include William Law's *A Serious Call to a Devout and Holy Life* (Westminster, 1955) and *The Journal of John Wesley* (Moody, n.d.).

The Modern World

As we approach the twentieth century, devotional literature becomes increasingly sentimentalized, divorced from the great themes of theology and addressed to the "heart" alone rather than the whole person. It consequently loses much of its power. The winnowing process of time has not yet been able to render its verdict on most of this material, but one entertains no great hopes that much of it will survive. But one rather eccentric figure from the nineteenth century deserves notice: the Jesuit poet Gerard Manley Hopkins. His energetic and innovative verse shines with the vision of a world "charged with the grandeur of God" and rings with the cry of a sensitive and intelligent soul wrestling with God in a search for spiritual reality: "Mine, Oh Thou Lord of Life, send my roots rain!"

One twentieth-century author merits a special section of his own as we conclude. The theological and apologetic works of C.S. Lewis abound in brilliant discussions of many of the issues we have addressed. "On the Reading of Old Books," *God in the Dock* (Eerdmans, 1970), pp. 200-207, is the most eloquent apology in existence for the kind of reading this essay recommends. *Miracles: A Preliminary Study* is the finest nontechnical study in print of the relationship between God and the natural world which makes petitionary prayer possible (Macmillan, 1947). *Letters to Malcolm: Chiefly on Prayer* is a book-length treatment of our general subject which is probably more thought-provoking than any other book on prayer (Harcourt Brace, 1963). But there are also the scintillating short essays: "Petitionary Prayer: A Problem Without an Answer," *Christian Reflections* (Eerdmans, 1967), pp. 142-51; "The Efficacy of Prayer," *The World's Last Night* (Harcourt Brace, n.d.), pp. 3-11; and "Work and Prayer," *God in the Dock*, pp. 104-107. Other pieces relevant but less directly related to our topic are too numerous to mention.

Finally, in a recent book I discuss the approach to reading this bibliographical essay has been recommending. In *Inklings of Reality: Essays Toward a Christian Philosophy of Letters* (Toccoa, GA: Toccoa Falls Press, 1996), I try to show how the right kind of reading of the Bible, the classics and the best of Christian writing as outlined above, can produce the kind of biblical consciousness and resulting wholeness of vision we need to live full and effective Christian lives.

Conclusion

The length of this bibliography may raise a fear lest reading become a substitute for prayer. It need not be so. Indeed, most of us could well do more of both. Most of the people I have cited were men who did; may we follow in their train.

Soli Deo Gloria.

Amen.

Appendix

Related Reviews

Editor's note: The review of *The Christian at Prayer* originally appeared in *The Journal of the Evangelical Theological Society*, 32:2 (June 1989), 280-81; a shorter version of the essay on Cranmer appeared in *Eternity*, September 1986, p. 17; and the review of Jeffrey's *A Burning and a Shining Light* appeared in *Eternity*, January 1988, p. 37

The Christian at Prayer: An Illustrated Prayer Manual Attributed to Peter the Chanter, Medieval and Renaissance Texts and Studies, no. 44. Ed. Richard C. Trexler (Binghamton, NY: Center for Medieval and Early Renaissance Studies, 1987). 260 pp., $25.00.

Petrus Cantor was one of the leading Parisian scholars of the last quarter of the twelfth century. He is chiefly remembered for works on practical ethics such as the *Verbum Abbreviatum*, a treatise on the virtues and vices (available in Migne's *Patriologia Latina* 205, cols. 21-554) and on sacramental theology (e.g. *Summa de Sacramentis*, edited by J.A. Dugauquier for the *Analecta Mediaevalia Namurcensia* in 1954). A large work previously existing only in manuscript was his *De Penitentia et Partibus Eius* (Of Penitence and Its Parts), one book of which, *De Oratione et Speciebus Illis*, has now been edited for modern readers by Trexler as *The Christian at Prayer*.

Literally titled "Concerning Prayer and Its Kinds," the book offers some fascinating insights into one medieval view of prayer. The Chanter analyzes prayer by the various bodily postures of the supplicant, viewed as expressing states of the soul. Prayer is defined as *dei benivolentie captatio*, "capturing the benevolence of God." In order to be effective the prayer must be pronounced slowly and distinctly, the supplicant must be able to remember what he has said, and the postures must be performed correctly (no cheating on those that may be physically uncomfortable or humiliating).

Like much medieval theology, the *De Oratione* is a curious blend of wisdom and utter nonsense. There is something crassly pragmatic and mechanical about the whole approach that leaves an almost impious taste in the mouth, and that, it seems to me, ultimately goes back to the problematic central concept of prayer as *captatio*. No one single word better captures the whole deadening thread of synergism (i.e., grace plus works) which runs through pre-Reformation theology and keeps it from grasping the biblical motifs of *sola gratia* (grace alone) and *sola fide* (faith alone)—as if God's grace were something that had to be or could be "seized" by our performance.

This concept of *captatio* even enables the Chanter to marvel at the paradox that *homo dum orat est quasi maior domini* because *homo, qui nihil est respectu creatori, imperat deo*: "Man while he prays is almost greater than the Lord," because "although with respect to the fact that he is a creature he is nothing, yet then he commands God." If his posture and pronunciation are good enough, he can make God do things—like transforming the elements of the Eucharist into the body and blood of Christ. (Is there any real difference in essence between this and some modern "word-faith" and "health-and-wealth" theologians?) Though the Chanter is aware that he is speaking, as it were, as a fool in his efforts to exalt prayer, his hyperbole is consistent with a view of prayer that is close to magic and a view of God that is tantamount to blasphemy.

And yet, having said all this, I would still recommend the *De Oratione* as a book not just for scholars interested in the history of doctrine but also for Christians interested in prayer. Though elements of the kind of theologizing that made the Reformation necessary have left their mark heavily upon the text, it also contains profound insights at precisely the points where many modern Christians tend to be naive. Its insistence that posture and pronunciation matter is rooted in bad theology but also in good psychology. If others pick up from our body language signs of our attitudes which either confirm or contradict our words, than surely God is able to read such signs as well. It may be that indifference to whether one kneels, prostrates himself or stands with raised hands in particular contexts of prayer signals a lack of involvement in what we are doing; it may be that a tolerance for multitudinous inarticulate "uhs," the use of "Lord" or "Father" after every phrase and other vain repetitions signifies a certain laxness in our own approach.

It should be remembered that Peter's emphasis on correct pronunciation and on being able to re-member what one has said was aimed partly at keeping people in a liturgical church from merely going through the motions. If our theology of prayer has risen from *captatio* to communion, our practice of that communion is sometimes guilty of a superficiality which would have astonished the Chanter.

Trexler provides a detailed introduction to Pe-ter the Chanter's work and the manuscript tradi-tion behind his edition. Petrus Cantor's Latin is not overly difficult. Only an occasional word can-not be found in a standard student's dictionary, and much of it is fairly smooth sailing for anyone who has (or even used to have) a moderate compe-tence in the language. For students of medieval theology or for anyone wishing to dust off his Latin with something less predictable than the Vulgate but not as stiff as Vergil, *The Christian at Prayer* is a book worth owning.

Dossier: Thomas Cranmer

Few lives that have profoundly influenced the history of the Church are more open to misunderstanding than that of Thomas Cranmer, archbishop of Canterbury under Henry VIII and principal architect of The Book of Common Prayer. The impact of his work is undeniable: Not only did it help to lay the groundwork for that great flowering of English Protestant piety in Spenser, George Herbert, John Donne, etc., but the sonorous strains of his English are still to be heard in the traditional wedding ceremony borrowed by countless denominations from its original Anglican context. Yet his involvement in "the great matter of the king's divorce" makes it easy to dismiss him as a mere political tool of Henry VIII who happened to have a gift for liturgical compromise and high-sounding prose. But such an evaluation of Cranmer would be as great an injustice as some of the more disreputable deeds of his infamous master.

Born in 1489, Cranmer was educated at Cambridge, where he learned from the new humanism of Colet and Erasmus a profound respect for the actual language of Scripture, as opposed to the scholastic subtleties erected upon it by the older medieval scholarship. Here, as so often, the Renaissance paved the way for the Reformation. Cranmer anticipated a quiet academic career, as he was elected fellow of Jesus College and proceeded to the doctorate in divinity. By nature a methodical and cautious thinker, he was not the man to jump on the latest bandwagon or easily espouse radical ideas. But already his love for Scripture was giving him a certain sympathy with some of Dr. Luther's "new" teaching, a sympathy which would slowly but surely grow throughout his career into a consistent and balanced belief in the major principles of the Reformation.

But Cranmer was not to be allowed to develop those views at leisure in the peaceful academic surroundings he loved. The king wanted to divorce his wife in order to marry Anne Boleyn, and he needed an archbishop who would support him in the affair. Cranmer had opposed the original marriage to Catherine of Aragon in the first place, believing that the Pope had no right to suspend the biblical injunction against marrying one's brother's wife. So to everyone's surprise (including his own), Thomas Cranmer was installed as archbishop of Canterbury on March 30, 1533. By April 23rd he had declared the marriage to Catherine void. Unfortunately, Henry's marital maneuvering did not end there, and so Cranmer found himself in what one might call the seamier side of the English Reformation.

Cranmer had never sought such preferment, and in fact actively resisted it. Henry stated more than once that he kept Cranmer around because he was the only man who was actually sincere in his advocacy. Cranmer was somewhat naive about power politics, and he ended up having to do some things for Henry which he found distasteful.

But he also used the influence of his office to

further the legitimately spiritual side of the Reformation in ways which could not have happened without him. In 1537 he introduced the first English Bible into the churches (Tyndale's work as completed by Coverdale). Under Henry and then Edward VI he worked slowly but surely for reform in doctrine and worship. The Second Prayer Book of 1552 and the Forty-Two Articles of 1553 were the culmination of his efforts. They committed the English church unmistakably to the Reformation, but with a light touch: Cranmer kept as much of the old familiar order of worship as he could while thoroughly removing specific Romanist doctrine and abuses. It was his love for the Bible as a concrete text, his commitment to the Reformation gospel of justification by faith alone and the humility which allowed him to pursue reform without contempt for the old, as much as his unsurpassed ear for the balanced and dignified phrase, which gave his work its enduring value.

It could not have seemed enduring to him. One month after the publication of the Forty-Two Articles, Edward died and Bloody Mary came to the throne, determined to return England to the Roman fold. Cranmer watched his life's work undone, his friends tortured and killed or exiled and himself committed to prison. Perhaps in despair, he became the only Marian martyr to sign a recantation. But he recovered his courage and went to the stake, holding first into the flames the offending hand which had signed that dastardly confession. We may believe that from the ramparts of heaven he had the satisfaction of seeing his work become the basis of the Elizabethan settlement which still underlies much of our Protestant worship tradition.

—————————

A Burning and a Shining Light: English Spirituality in the Age of Wesley. Ed. David Lyle Jeffrey (Grand Rapids, MI: Eerdmans, 1987). 517 pp., $16.95.

"We live in an age of small things," wrote D. Martyn Lloyd-Jones of the state of contemporary spirituality. And no wonder: for Lloyd-Jones was a man who immersed himself in the spirituality of the Puritan fathers and of the great revivals of the past, especially that of the first Great Awakening in the eighteenth century. *A Burning and a Shining Light* reveals the reasons for Lloyd-Jones' assessment. It is an anthology of spiritual writings— hymns, sermons, letters, essays, meditations—by a representative sample of the men and women who were mightily used by God in that first Great Awakening in England. The famous—Isaac Watts, William Law, the Wesleys, Whitefield, John Newton, Wilberforce—and the more forgotten—Elizabeth Singer Rowe, Philip Doddridge, Hannah Moore, John Fletcher—give eloquent testimony to the work of the Holy Spirit in what must be counted the true "enlightenment" of the eighteenth century.

Jeffrey edits the selections, modernizing with a

light touch which makes the reading easier while preserving the true spirit of the originals, and provides biographical introductions for each writer and a brief historical introduction to the whole period.

Two crucial truths will be brought home to those who read this book. The first is how far we are from a true state of revival today, despite many claims to the contrary. Shining from the pages of each of these writers is a single-minded earnestness and integrity, a purity of intention in the search for God, whose absence becomes painfully obvious when one turns to even the best Christian literature of our own day.

The second truth is the possibility of revival even in such an age of spiritual decadence as our own. Jeffrey's introduction is one of the finest short pieces of historical writing I have read in a long time. In it he draws a portrait of the spiritual darkness which had enveloped England before the Revival which reads like a precise delineation of our own vices. For liberalism there was Deism; for drugs there was rum; for abortion with its degradation of human life there was the slave trade, just as entrenched and with similar consequences for the whole moral tone of the nation. And then as now there was a large mass of nominal and hopelessly compromised Christianity which was more a part of the problem than the solution. There was as little prospect of real revival then as there is today. But it was in just such a time of darkness that God began one of His greatest works of renewal.

Scripture Index

Index of Names and Subjects